Circumference of Me

of

Book and cover design by Stan Nelson

Circumference of Me

Steve Burnett and George S. Smith

Acknowledgements

Circumference of Me is the result of two lifetimes of work—one in mainly rural settings, the other in The No. 1 World City, New York. The diverse backgrounds of the authors solidified their belief that "management is management" regardless of setting, educational background, or number of co-workers. Great managers are in every profession, from the largest of companies to the smallest of non-profit associations, from the smallest of school districts to metropolitan student-cities.

The diverse paths taken that led to the writing of *Circumference of Me* emphasize the importance of business mentors and corporate devils, and the important lessons each handed down in the daily exercise of duties.

There are too many of these extraordinary people to single out and thank for the lessons—good and bad—they administered. But to them all: Thank you! Your example made us better than we could have been on our own.

Special thanks to Stan Nelson, an extraordinary editor and grammarian. His insight, attention to detail, suggestions, and edits made this effort better than it was—and better than the authors could have possibly made it.

What they say:

Just when you thought you had seen the latest and greatest message about what steps people need to take to become great managers, along comes *Circumference of Me*.

If you have read other books on management theory or practice, fine, but you need to read this one. It has been my pleasure to work with both authors on projects ranging from global communications to brand awareness to internal and external communications practices. They do not just talk a good game; they know their business.

Consider yourself warned: This is not your typical management book. *Circumference of Me* is about … you.

It does not present the safe-at-all-costs, practical side of corporations, management practices, and expected behaviors for employees. There is no do-this-or-else business theory included, nor are there the predictable management truisms speckled with visual word-posters designed to build Spirit, Enthusiasm, Motivation, Optimism, or Team Building.

Circumference of Me will give you a view of the various steps necessary to rise to the challenges of being a manager—or a better manager—and create the environment for you to realize your potential through its unique presentation and content.

Joe Ford
Former Chairman and CEO, Alltel Corp.
Partner, Westrock Capital Partners

Circumference of Me is a classic example of pull/push marketing. Most of us know—or think we do—what we want and who we are; it is the stopping to look and the prompting and pulling out of us that is usually needed more than the simple act of pushing an idea into us.

There is a fine line between teaching and shaping someone's under-standing and motivating their will to act. I believe an effective teacher has to do both and there is a nice balance in the lessons of this book.

There are two words to describe this book: Fresh and creative. The illustrations are directly connected to the writing and help the reader create a mental image.

Circumference of Me has many mini-lessons about life and about business, to not only think about, but to remember and use.

This book creates a pathway to dream about things that really stir us up and make us better at what we do and not just create traditional goals. Encouraging that in people is very important and *Circumference of Me* shouts that message loud and clear.

Kevin Dial
Director of Operations,
CBIZ Medical Management Professionals

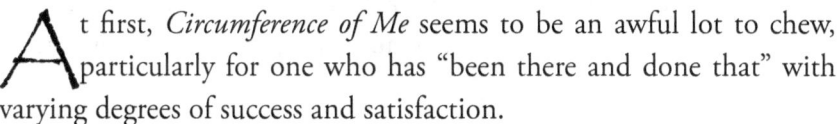

At first, *Circumference of Me* seems to be an awful lot to chew, particularly for one who has "been there and done that" with varying degrees of success and satisfaction.

It was hard for me to want to let go of one thought and move on to the next. This is not a criticism, rather validation of the idea that "It's not a goal…it's a mission, so it's the journey that counts."

Smith and Burnett have found a way to draw the reader into their concept of management philosophy without a bunch of guideposts. Instead, the reader enters as a wanderer and quickly finds himself en-gaged.

John Trotti
Editor
Grading & Excavation *magazine*

As schools have sought to meet the public demand for more accountability, educators have searched for ways to merge the principles of management in the business world with that of the educational realm. During 40-plus years as an educator and administrator I have read numerous "management" books and had yet to find one that could be so applicable to the educational community.

Circumference of Me is an exception to this. Building upon the principle of self-development and the dynamics of relationships, the authors have managed to connect the principles of business while reflecting the central component of effective educational institutions: First, you teach the child. Without knowing and being comfortable with oneself, an educator cannot reach the heart of a student. The ability to have effective interpersonal skills impacts and extends beyond the classroom to the staff, parents, and community.

The whimsical drawings are wonderful for those who need more than the written word to grasp the total meaning of the thought. As with any good piece of children's literature, the illustrations should reflect the words of the author. The drawings by Steve Burnett are more than illustrations; they are intuitive and thought-provoking in and of themselves.

Circumference of Me is an easy-to-read book, perfect for those who feel rushed, with great application to those in the field of education.

Bobbie Jean McCarty Thurman
Elementary Principal (retired)
Commerce (Texas) Independent School District

Welcome to the world of George Smith and Steve Burnett—where whimsy consistently opens the door to profound and practical insights.

Burnett crafts illustrations that are simple yet stunning, capturing the essence of chapters in minimal brush strokes. Smith paints word pictures like few others can, exploring life circumstances from a unique and insightful perspective.

The chapter-ending takeaways offer common sense that is, unfortunately, far too uncommon in business and government today.

Just read it. Put it into practice. You will be glad you did.

John Wallace

Retired Director - Verizon Communications

Table of Contents

Unconventional Wisdom

Processed Advice

Foreword

Each chapter of *Circumference of Me* is written and illustrated with someone just like you in mind: a person who wants to explore realistically the depths of his or her abilities—not only to think about realities, but also about perceptions and how they influence your life, both personally and professionally.

Circumference of Me is designed to help you improve your business self, to enhance your understanding of your leadership abilities and how to expand them, to help you realize the synergies that become possible when your business and personal lives are in sync, and to guide you to achieve success and personal fulfillment in whatever business you choose.

It doesn't matter whether you own your business or occupy a square in a corporation's organizational chart, or even if you are just starting out at either. You will take away something positive from *Circumference of Me*.

Whether you peruse the Contents page or check out the fifty-seven individual chapter headings, you will be able to identify quickly the subjects that interest you at this point in your career, and find ideas and thoughts that speak directly to you in *Circumference of Me*. And you will ask yourself:

Why did this chapter heading interest me?

What is the intent of the chapter and how can I use it?

Will this chapter give me advice to advance my career? Make me a better employee? Better manager?

What was the take-away lesson?

Would that work in my organization?

What would people think if I tried that at work?

Circumference of Me is not a cure-all for the Business Blahs, and it can only be one among many influences and counsels that help in your business and personal lives. Its chapters give you principles to be remembered and used when you need them. *Circumference of Me* is designed to help you to think about your business world, and to explore different options that can take you to success.

Circumference of Me's mixture of unique visuals, around-the-corner word images, and ideas and concepts gleaned from the experiences of successful managers and leaders encourages you think about *you* in a different way. The ideas, thoughts, real-life examples, and advice in these pages are guides to help you find and build various pathways for success and satisfaction.

Using what you learn, you can gather errant pieces of your professional life, even if they've been shattered by failure or unforeseen calamity, and rebuild—or create—a *Circumference of Me*, your own atmosphere of solid principles.

The challenge is to think and learn; the challenge is accepting; the challenge is in your personal ability to look at yourself analytically and, where necessary, to change what needs changing in your personal *Circumference of Me*.

Circumference
of Me

1 • Yes, you have a 'circumference'

You probably don't think about having a "circumference." But you do have one. Every man, woman, and child has a personal circumference, defined by culture, education, basic personality, life lessons (learned, ignored, or forgotten), hopes and fears.

Your *Circumference of Me* is what makes you—well, *you*. Its circle defines you as a person, both professionally and personally; it's your aura, your persona. It's the outward focus of the inner you. It is the public face you allow others to see. It dictates how they perceive you in the common slice of the world you share.

Your circumference is not made up of one specific trait, or any number of them. It's made of every single personality trait, and includes every single thing you have done to get to this point in your life. It's the circle that connects to your *past* and embraces your *now*, with both working together to define your *future*.

And your circumference is more than a personal inventory of attributes and weaknesses. It isn't something you meditate upon to pass

Contemplate the circumference of you.

2

Ideal business scenario: Students become teachers.

the time. To know your circumference is to define your life, to be conscious of who you are and what you want to be during different segments of your life journey.

When was the last time you contemplated your *Circumference of Me?* That's not a trick question. Determining your personal circumference is necessary because it's not a goal. It's a mission.

That mission calls for an objective evaluation of every aspect that makes you a unique person. That evaluation should lead you to recognize the sharp corners in the personal and business brief that defines you, and to devise an aggressive action plan to round off those obtrusive corners, creating a smooth surface that projects not only the aura, but the reality of your life. Attaining a *Circumference of Me* puts into clear focus (or at least "un-raggeds" the edges of) your professional appearance, competence in any situation, calm demeanor, and extraordinary communication skills. Given the right situation, and the right projection of self, it instills in your co-workers a belief in your virtual invincibility.

People who evaluate and then refine their *Circumference of Me* achieve simplicity of action. They transform from employees and managers who are in learning mode to managers who mentor and teach.

So you have a *Circumference of Me*—a robust, simple container that holds all the variegated elements that make up *you* in the *now*. You decide whether just to watch your container shrink or stagnate, or to take actions to help it grow. You elect to use life experiences and new-found wisdom to change the elements that make up its unique shape. What you do with your *Circumference* is strictly up to you. No one but you can create an environment for personal change, set the amount of change, or delegate degrees of importance to changes.

It's difficult to be aware of your personal *Circumference*, your boundaries, your length and breadth and depth—your personal and professional periphery. However, it's important to understand that the boundaries of your *Circumference of Me* were not established by chance. They were set by *you*. No one else gets the credit—or the blame.

The following chapters are intended to aid you on your journey to realize your *Circumference of Me*, and expand your potential for expanding and improving it.

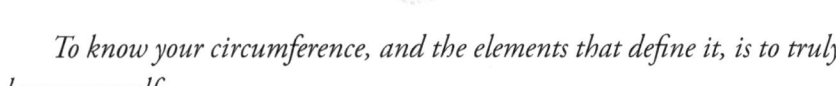

To know your circumference, and the elements that define it, is to truly know yourself.

Your personal business circumference changes as you change.

2 • Positives from negatives

There are times in your life when things stop making sense. Familiar sights and sounds seem out of focus and muffled; systems which only yesterday were comforters in your business, educational structure, non-profit association, or corporate world miraculously turn into a patchwork quilt with a Drunkard's Path design. Policies which once seemed to protect you are suddenly, like the cat of homespun legend, stealing your breath away and smothering your creativity.

When your personal world—your professional portrait, familiar processes at home and work, predictable market trends—breaks apart, take comfort in the fact that there are always pieces left. Don't discard those pieces; they are parts of *you*. Take them and play with them. Put them together to create a new picture of the change in you—a *you* collage.

To do that, take a giant step in the direction of change: Put your brain in neutral. Of course, that's hard to do. Your brain does not normally recognize commands to go into neutral mode because there

Sometimes when something ...

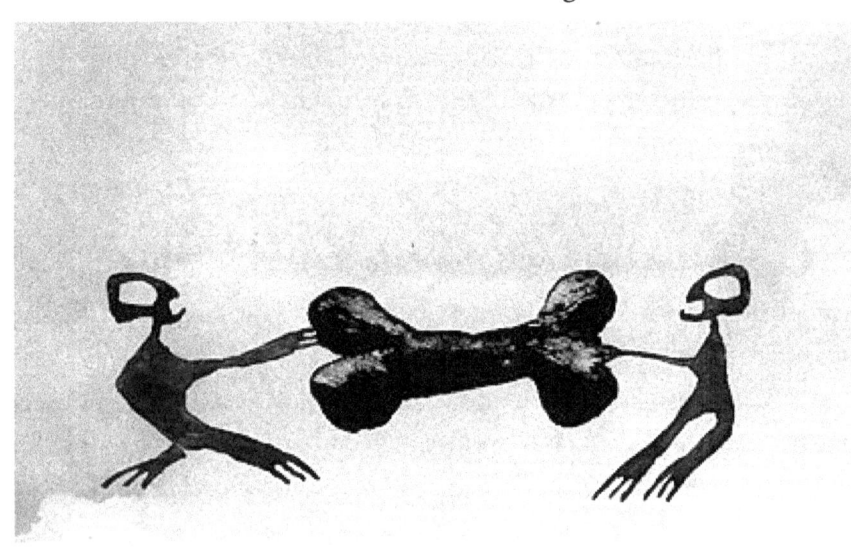

seems to be no sense to it. With your brain in neutral, there are no thought patterns being created, and the brain is a pattern-loving organ. Your thinking self yearns to make sense of events, people, and opportunities; it wants to reason its way out of an economic ditch, a

... is broken, the pieces are ...

catastrophic relationship, or a job that truly sucks.

Putting your brain in neutral does not mean "not thinking." It means *selectively* thinking about things that, when viewed from the perspective of your personal or professional life, are "neutral."

... better than the whole.

One manager confides that her personal neutral mode consists of closing her eyes during a quiet moment and concentrating on a single thought: A turtle walking at the edge of a tranquil pond. In a personal form of meditation or bio-feedback, the woman simply takes a minute or less and "walks" the turtle in her mind—silently repeating, "Turtle, turtle, turtle," matching each step. This form of "non-sense" calms and relaxes this particular manager, enabling her to put her creative brain in neutral, giving her thoughts a brief, but refreshing pause.

It's the paradox of non-sense. Through this neutral process, or whatever one you create, it's possible to direct your brain back to Square One, then take off again in a search for new patterns and conclusions. Now is as good a time as any to explode yourself with that mental dynamite and reinvent *you*. It's the perfect time for reinvestment of creative energy, setting new goals, dreaming new dreams, strengthening your personal will, and rearranging your personal organizational structure to find positive uses for those tired, old, broken, and scattered pieces of the truisms of your yesterday.

When things break—in your personal life, in your job, in the market—huge amounts of negative and positive energy are released. That energy has to go somewhere. You choose where to direct that energy. Doesn't it make sense to use it to enhance the positive side of your life?

That's the premise and reason for the *Circumference of Me*—directing stray thoughts into a living, breathing, growing example of how you can change your life through the new awareness, appreciation and development of a very special personal tool: personal thought leadership.

Take charge of your thoughts. Take charge of your life.

3 • Know thyself

Who are you? Why are you doing what you're doing? Are you happy doing it, and, if not, again, why are you doing it?

Okay, so you work for a business or association and you have a five-word title, or aspire to have one—manager/senior manager/director/vice president of something and something. The company has you lined up to be on an MBO (management by objectives) bonus plan and, sometime in the future you may be eligible for a car allowance, stock options, and more.

You have arrived. Or plan to do so quickly.

Before you get too cocky, check your image in the mirror. Do you see an aura of success (regal purple with gold piping) around your body? A competent manager whose reassuring smile bespeaks volumes of positive accolades from co-workers and high-level management? Confidence you can sell by the pound?

Let's take it for granted: You are a confident manager. Your walk, talk, and mannerisms portray success for all to see.

Look at me! Please! Now! I am the picture of success! If not quite yet, soon!

But, confidence aside, you have weaknesses. If that comes as a revelation, you are already in trouble. Everyone has weaknesses.

If you were asked to name your top five weaknesses—personal or professional traits that could keep you from climbing the tenuous business ladder more than a few more rungs—what might they be? Have you giv-

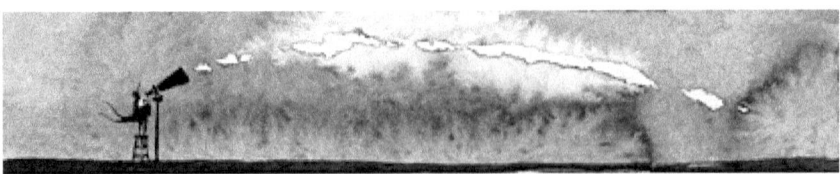

If your idea is a good one ... will you let it be known?

en any thought to your weaknesses and, if so, are you confident enough to name them aloud? (And in a room with a closed door doesn't count.)

More importantly, do others—co-workers, supervisors, top management—know your weaknesses? Do they hope you have what it takes to minimize them, or turn them into strengths? Are they waiting for you to overcome them? Or do they simply not care one way or the other?

Far too many managers don't take the time or have the inclination to focus on the traits that carved the career path to their present positions. And those same managers usually are not interested in the kind of self-analysis that will help them to determine whether those traits can get them to their personal and professional goals.

To attain success, self-analysis is not only a fundamental rite of passage—it is a necessity. There is nothing tougher for a person than self-analysis. To many, the mere suggestion may be as scary as thinking about sliding naked down a giant razor blade.

Some psychologists claim an objective self-analysis is impossible. It is in their best interests to think so, and to promote that premise. They are right in one respect: there are people who can't see their own weaknesses; therefore, they don't believe they exist. Such people are wrong—but then, they are the people who won't admit they make mistakes, either.

While it is an extremely uncomfortable undertaking, looking at yourself in the psyche mirror with an objective eye is possible. It takes a strong heart, a stronger will, a solid mind, an enhanced sense of self-worth, and an understanding of how stripping away one's personal veneer can be a cathartic experience—not an embarrassing one.

Take a chance. Strip away your veneer and see what lies beneath.

Spend the time and make an emotional commitment to analyze yourself before someone with a bigger title does it for you.

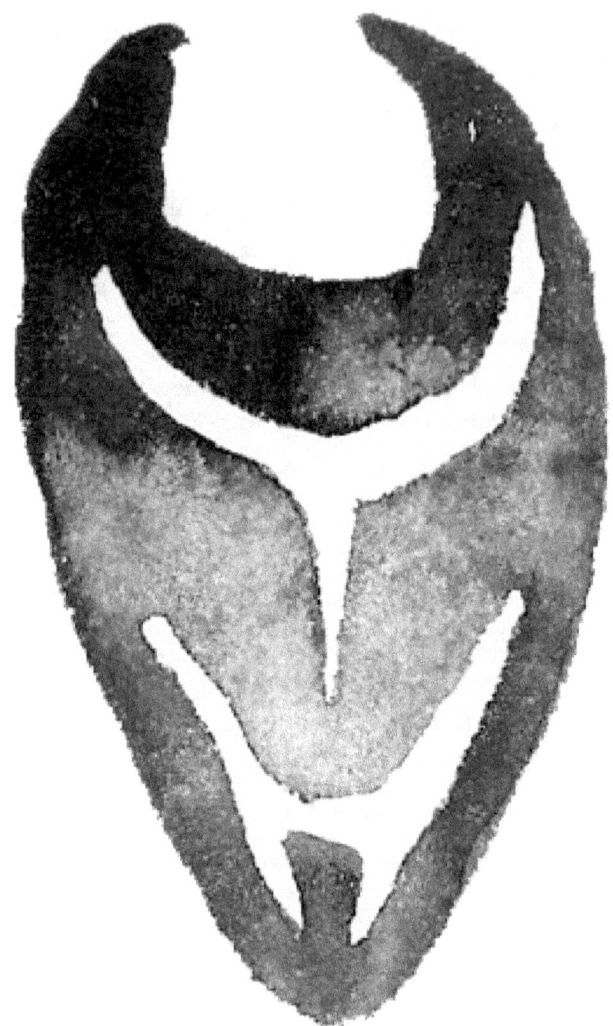

4 • You're terrified? Good!

Whether you are just starting off on your career journey or you have been a long-time employee, you may think every day that you are living on the edge of your abilities. You're not.

Growth is rarely gained by standing on solid ground.

If you are like the huge majority of workers, you are ensconced inside a mile-wide comfort zone, not daring to step near the edges of your experience and abilities.

You may not recognize it, but your abilities will not grow, and the impact and importance of your experiences will shrink *unless* and *until* you take the necessary steps to live on the edge. Taking steps—even tiny, baby steps—past the edge of your self-imposed comfort zone is absolutely necessary for your personal and professional growth.

You know why you don't venture closer to the edge. It's your fear of failure—of biting off more than you can chew, of not gathering moss on your personal rolling stone, and a bevy of other shallow-water clichés. Fear of failure is not fatal, but it's also not conducive to progress among the office ranks.

If you feel you are watching the life drain out of your frame of opportunity—your abilities aren't growing and the value of your experience is shrinking—then you have two choices:

• Step back into more familiar surroundings and possibly stifle unseen opportunities, or

• Step closer to the fearsome edge and get sucked away into a whole new universe of opportunity.

Of course, such a prospect is frightening. The unknown always is. We all want to know what's behind the veil of uncertainty in business or in life. Once you set foot in uncharted territory, you are where your hitherto accepted limits aren't accepted, anymore.

It's a time for reflection, reviewing old goals and setting new ones, and working to mesh your unspoken dreams with your new reality. You have faced your fears and taken decisive action to change what is within your power to change.

You are not the same person you were before you made a conscientious decision to actively seek change. Without experimentation, without exploring the depths of your potential, without expanding your knowledge base and business acumen, you cannot climb higher on the success ladder.

You will be doomed to hang precariously to the one safe rung or slide ever downward.

That which terrifies you also creates an opportunity for growth.

5 • Professional you vs. personal you

Every aspiring manager should remember this simple axiom: There is life after work.

Consider three ingredients that have nothing to do with work, yet are absolutely necessary for a successful career: Family, friends, and downtime.

Family support during one's rise in the corporate ranks is crucial to making the various transitions as smooth as possible. Work can be all-consuming, if you let it. But it cannot hug you, or listen to your thoughts, aspirations, and fears. Work cannot ruffle your hair playfully, just to let you know someone cares.

Of course, you have friends at work. If you don't, work can become drudgery and make long days even longer. And while there's nothing wrong with having friends who jump the boundary from work to after-work, from a psychological point of view, it is important to have

Workplace friends are one reason to show up each day.

friends who have nothing to do with work. Relaxing with friends from work presents two potential "uh-ohs": 1) The subject of work will come up, and 2) with no outside influences, ideas or observations, the flow of creative juices can be greatly inhibited.

Downtime is essential to clear, concise reasoning. Smart managers realize this small truth and make sure they take time off to re-energize. Many top-level managers make time to leave work behind on a regular basis. The ones who understand the value of time away from work always return with new ideas to create a better company. Their creativity is an offshoot of time away from the day-to-day chores that always abound in the modern company.

Your work world will survive if you are not available for a time for e-mail, phone calls or text messages. Truly, it will. Those who believe otherwise will forever be banished to Office Hell.

Unconditional
Wisdom

6 • The No. 1 management tool

I t's time to do an itemized check of your professional tool belt. Education (regular classroom or Street Smart U.)? *Check.* Experience? *Check (Or soon will have, or working on it).*

"We have seen the enemy and he is us."—Pogo

Strong work ethic? *Check.*

Ability to work well with others? *Check.*

Ready acceptance of any task, and ability to deliver satisfactory results on time and under budget? *Check (When circumstances allow).*

So, what's the problem? Why does your personal corporate vehicle seem stalled, or your fast-track career slowed down, like a tractor-trailer rig straining up a mountain highway? Are your beliefs realistic about where you are and where you should be? If you are young, eager, and impatient, probably not. If you are older, and have started questioning your abilities and blaming others for your status, another glance at the mirror will show you the problem.

Have you done everything you can do to get where you want to go in the time you wanted it to take to get there?

What do you think is the No. 1 tool that every great manager has at the ready at all times?

A great education and a high GPA? *Can't hurt, but in some cases your supervisor may have made it on a high school diploma.*

Superb work ethic? *Good, but that's a given for up-and-comers.*

Willing to do whatever it takes to get the job done? *Okay, but see "Superb work ethic."*

Profit-oriented? *A good tool to have in the belt, but it's a Catch-22. You can't get what you don't have without having the wherewithal to get it. How do you get the experience you need to be profit-oriented without getting the experience?*

Good communication skills? *Absolutely essential, but not the main driver.*

Brown-nosing without getting your proboscis dirty? *Oh, shut up!*

Well, what about *time management?*

One of the hardest things for managers to learn, and to learn to use to maximize efficiency and productivity is time management.

Let's accept that there's not enough time to do all the tasks assigned to you. On top of that, you get seventy to eighty e-mails a day, each requiring some time and many demanding even more time. If you don't take the time to read and answer them, then you're a jerk, a slacker, a goldbrick, a drone waiting around for retirement, or have a colossal don't-give-a-damn attitude. If you are a high-level manager and don't make the time to answer e-mail queries, you are a snobbish *jerque*. So you lose time to take care of the e-mail deluge.

But think: Your e-mail volume is just a percentage of what your boss gets, and his or hers is just a percentage of what the next level of management gets, and so on. If you are swamped with e-mails, that does not bode well for those higher up the corporate ladder.

Still, some great managers make it a conscientious practice to answer every single e-mail from every single employee, every dealer, every student, and every customer or potential customer.

Aspiring managers—those who want to lead rather than perpetually follow—must quickly learn what those great managers know, whether dealing with piles of tasks or e-mails: the not-so-subtle art of time management.

Learn the two "izes": Itemize and prioritize. Make a list of projects and tasks, prioritize them according to relative importance, and cross-index them to take into account deadlines and available resources. The items you can do quickly, or for which you can do your assigned part and pass on down the line, should be at the top of the list.

And be sure to answer those e-mails.

Here's why: A president and CEO of a large technology company admits that answering e-mails takes a huge bite out of his workday. But he knows if he wants to be a leader, he has to make time—in a word, prioritize his acknowledgment of the concerns of others—to show people how important they are to the company.

What could be more important to a leader?

Learn and adhere to the principles of time management in your life and work, and you will control your destiny.

7 • Business bugaboos

A trio of business bugaboos derails more projects, more careers, and more companies than all other factors combined: Ego, turf and titles.

Let's deal with ego first, and get one thing straight, quick: Every successful manager in history has had a strong ego and sense of self. Every one understood and appreciated the necessary boundaries of division of labor within a company, and all tried to mesh their operations or project goals with the company's mission. Every single one of them sought advancement in the corporate ranks.

Having a strong ego is part of the development and makeup of every successful manager. But having a big ego is not the same as having confidence in one's abilities or the ability to view one's accomplishments and potential in a realistic spotlight. It's a fact that many managers are not as good as they think they are. Many sell their attributes short, and many potentially great managers have not developed the attitude or temperament to believe in their own abilities.

A strong ego, tempered by realism, is priceless for a steady, uphill climb on any professional ladder. But developing an ego as a positive personality trait, like the making of a fine wine, must be done under strict parameters, with little room for experimentation.

***

Confidence is just another word for ego ... minus the obnoxious gene.

8 • Turf: the legends of warlords

A major failing among mid-level managers is an inability to see beyond their personal, self-imposed boundary lines. Thinking, "I am in charge of this project, and I will control it," is simply wrong-headed. Each department is a part that exists to assist other parts so the corporate engine can run smoothly and efficiently.

Turf protectionism was common among ancient warlords and still is practiced by nations or regions run by tribal chiefs. There are no successful companies among which turf warfare is tolerated. There is nothing worse in a business than a "virus"—a virulent strain of egotism—created by the ministrations and manipulations of quarreling corporate warlords.

Managers who adhere to the archaic practice of turf protection, to the detriment of the company, will not be around to see necessary changes unfold.

While "turf" is strictly a boundary issue and a sincere bugaboo in the constant search for corporate success, a manager's "territory" should be scrutinized constantly for expansion possibilities—not in the sense of "securing more territory" to feel important, but to improve the internal processes that benefit the company. In other words, how can one department help other departments in ways individual managers may not have even contemplated? And how do you accomplish that without offending the boundary issues of other managers?

Overtures must be presented in terms of mutual consideration and benefit.

"I was thinking about that interesting project you mentioned last week and how it could help the company. What if my department assisted you by . . . ?"

There is an example of the absolute best that communication and camaraderie have to offer: A word of praise, followed by an offer of assistance.

Real life. Real, positive results.

If you want to expand your territory, do it for the right reasons. If you just want to be in charge of "more" simply to expand your turf, buy grass seed.

9 • Titles: goals drive ambitions

Great managers constantly search for ways for their efforts and the efforts of people in their department to help other departments and managers succeed for the good of the business.

Good managers become great managers by building coalitions through mutual respect, and offering assistance on common projects. Building a strong partnership on a single project can help you climb innumerable rungs on your career ladder.

Seeking a successive string of promotions and title enhancements is a sign of a focused manager. Managers only interested in bigger titles may get them, but they might be the only goals they attain, at the cost of greater and more valuable goals, like gaining deserved responsibility and respect through your ability to address challenges responsibly. Gain those goals, and your titles will come.

It's always lonely atop a self-constructed pedestal.

Great managers never let their egos, turfs or quests for titles interfere with the primary goal of corporate wellness.

A title is only as good as the character of the person who holds it.

A mixture of a strong grasp of reality, helpful spirit, and strong work ethic pour the foundation for a strong corporate career.

10 • See the C's. Be the C's

There are three C's that managers take to the Everyday Business Bank: Cooperation, coordination, communication.

A survey of the world's top corporate managers would reveal startling similarities among their management techniques. Without exception, even if they use different words in different ways with different emphasis, all would agree that the Three C's are the defining differences between passable managers and ones destined to be remembered as difference-makers.

Cooperation embraces ideas that come from other people and other departments or organizations, and their value. It is not a simple give-and-take action, but a give-and-*receive* method of operation with far-ranging benefits. The very basis of cooperation is two-way communication—it binds groups and individuals to a central project.

Dream the dream. Harness the Three C's to create your own reality.

Little is gained by creating balanced inertia.

Coordination between the same entities deepens the personal, intellectual, and corporate relationships between them. One group's success hinges on the actions of the other group's participants. It is the corporate equivalent of the group hug.

By now, you can tell the most important of the three C's is positive and uplifting *communication.*

Far too many projects die horrible, screaming deaths; far too many careers crash and burn; far too many companies suffer because of people's inability to talk to other people.

Regardless of your charismatic qualities, personal commitment to success, basic leadership abilities, vision, creativity, or multi-tasking acumen, you cannot become a great manager without the ability to accurately convey ideas to others, paint word images that easily can be seen by others, or effectively communicate verbally or with the written word.

If you are not an accomplished communicator, don't sit around and whine internally about your shortcoming. Do something about it. Take a business communications course from a local college or university, or online. Read recommended books about leadership, manage-

Maximize results by maximizing efforts to reach the same goals.

ment, and effective communication techniques.

Be proactive about communication, one of the most important of all management traits.

While sheer will and determination can perform miracles, those attributes only have short-term value. Even the most gifted leader cannot be successful without working for, with, and through others. As a matter of undisputed fact, there is no one-person major company.

Even the Lone Ranger had Tonto.

Don't get distracted. Keep your eye on the goal.

11 • Tunnel vision with eyes wide open

Just like the whaler who is so proud of his vigilance for his prey, all the time unaware that he has been plying his trade from atop a humpback, too many managers firmly believe tunnel vision is an admirable trait, useful for every project.

It never has been, is not today, and never will be. Tunnel vision—an accepted way to see projects that must be viewed and worked on with blinders in shower-curtain position—is a specialized tool for a specific job and only should be put into action on special occasions of the short-term variety.

A seldom-recognized trait of great managers is the ability to focus on tasks at hand while at the same time developing the peripheral vision necessary to watch out for unexpected opportunities.

That's the hard part about being a see-all, do-everything manager:

keeping focused on critical, short-term tasks while maintaining the secondary focus required to look around corners, over hillocks, behind obstacles, and past the horizon.

Focus, yet see beyond the obvious.

See unseen opportunities while keeping your focus.

Be able to shift visual and cerebral focus on command, yet never lose sight of the task at hand. It's a trick that the world's best have mastered.

It can be a difference maker between being successful today or being successful today and tomorrow.

12 • The mind is a terrible thing in haste

Being able to work quickly can be a big help when that ability is combined with two definite attributes: accuracy and efficiency.

Unfortunately, "quick" and "sloppy" are more apt to be placed together in your personnel file than "quick" and "exceedingly accurate and productive."

Any employee can be quick. Moving that ability to a high level of competence, thereby increasing the confidence of higher-level managers in your abilities, is a life-long chore.

Honestly, workers who are normally quick and accurate do occasionally turn out some sloppy work that becomes evident in their final product or service.

You know you've done it, too: the quickly composed e-mail with an attachment—which was not attached; the report built from a template and the date the report was made was not changed; the expense report with a missing receipt; the e-mail you sent without stopping to check whether it went out to all recipients who should have been included in the information-dissemination chain.

As you enter your chosen profession, work to enhance your skills to be *accurate, efficient,* and *on time* before you combine those three with *quick.*

Refrain from poisoning your corporate profile with a quick response, of which the sole attribute is that you finished it in record time.

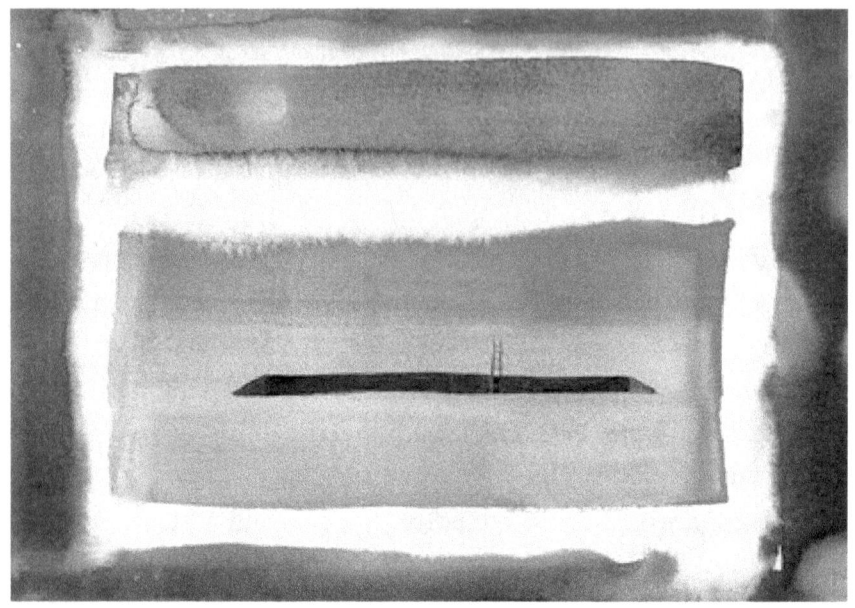

The proper height for a managerial ladder is one of perspective.

13 • Where's my ladder?

Ambition is like a ladder. Without two strong sides and rungs arranged at regular intervals, chances of a safe climb are very slim indeed.

Young managers want to scamper up the ambition ladder. The faster the pace, the better they like it. Seasoned managers, either patient and not in an unrealistic hurry to be put in a position that might expose their weaknesses, or who have decided later in their careers to tackle the climb, use each rung as a learning experience to assist them on their vertical climbs in their chosen professions.

Is there one route that is best? To each his own.

But on principle, each rung of a career ascension should be used as an opportunity to learn about your company and yourself.

A career should not be judged by how fast a person gets to a certain position, but what the person brings to the corporate table when placed in a decision-making role.

Whatever your pace, make it your ultimate goal to learn how to manage in a way that realizes the most efficiency and effective benefits for your company.

Find the company that you know is a good fit. Secure the ladder that fits your personality, abilities, and goals.

Then, climb, Baby, climb!

There's no elevator to the top of the ladder. It takes hard work and you need to be in shape to climb it.

Circumference of Me

Unconventional
Wisdom

Chores: Performing them well is the beginning that leads to successful careers.

14 • 'Tis better to shovel than bail

It is an old axiom, but a business truism just the same, that shit flows, rolls, or bounces downhill, depending on the individual consistency and age of said waste.

It's a fact of business life: You will have unimaginable and unimaginative chores to do in a corporate environment. There often are tough assignments that nobody wants to do, but almost everybody has to do.

The avalanches of shit you will face in business will be awe-inspiring—or downright scary. Learn to master and manage them, not to be buried by them, and to shovel shit with efficiency and aplomb. Learn to look over and past the piles to see the emergent light on the horizon.

Lesson 1: Accept shoveling shit as a rite of passage. Know that the company CEO was a Supreme Shit Shoveler in his day. Follow his or her example: Do your duty, shovel to the best of your ability, and move on.

Lesson 2: It's impossible to pick up a turd from the clean end. Grab it with both hands and dispose of it as quickly as possible.

15 • Handing the shovel to others

When asked or ordered to perform a shit-shoveling chore, you must approach it as an opportunity, not as an aversion. Shovel with alacrity. In doing so, you are preparing yourself for the next step in the evolutionary process of the business world. When you readily accept delegated chores, you prepare yourself to delegate to others.

The art of delegation must be learned. One cannot master it by osmosis. Neither is it a genetic attribute. Unfortunately, the only way to learn how not to micromanage every detail of a project (or just do it yourself) and to delegate instead is to become a manager or project leader and be in a position of *having* to depend on others.

The ability to delegate—to shift shit-shoveling to subordinates—is one of the hardest management skills for young managers (and many older, established managers) to learn. For one thing, it goes against the grains of egocentric managers and the personal preferences of many workers. Most good employees and a vast majority of managers— good, bad and in between—believe they can perform duties faster and get better results than anyone who works with them.

It's not necessarily true, but that doesn't make it any less so in their minds. Perceptions *are* realities.

If you truly want to become a corporate leader, you will have to move shit in various forms—liquid, clumps and hard, non-candy mountains—from one place to another for a time. In the Corporate Tribe, it's called paying your dues. Ante up!

Follow a few simple rules: Take a shit chore and do it to the best of your ability. Show what you can do by simply doing it. Make a niche for yourself that proves your value to the company.

Melvin sure does shovel shit well. And he does it without complaining!

If you are in a position of having to accept shit shoveled to you, and you are told to make something substantial out of it, make it the best pile of shit ever built in the history of the company.

Aspire to be a superb shit shoveler. In fact, be the freakin' King of Shit-Shoveling. Learn not only to shovel it in efficient, bite-size chunks, so to speak, but also how to use the exercise as a learning experience.

Few managers see the need or want to learn to be good shit shovelers. Most managers won't, but should, confide to subordinates why shit has to be shoveled, and how they fit into the shoveling channels. Few managers ever stop to tell a new employee: "Here's a chore. It's not glamorous; in fact, it's a shit chore. But it's important and here's why ..."

All new employees of any company should be versed in the practical reasons why shit flows downhill and how it is absolutely essential for aspiring executive managers to shovel it quickly and efficiently until there's no more to shovel. They should know that it's better to shovel shit than bitch and moan about having to do it, and let it build up until the only way to get rid of it is to bail.

Shit-shoveling should be viewed as a valuable lesson that should be embraced, figuratively, if not literally. Shoveling shit is a necessary part of the business process. It also is much better than the alternative—not having any shit to shovel, sitting home watching reruns of *Cops*, and glancing at the "Help Wanted" ads during commercials.

When it comes to paying your dues and shoveling your share of corporate shit, adopt the approach by Oliver Twist in the musical based on the Dickens novel: "Please, sir, may I have some more?"

16 • Mix business & monkey business

I t was the first day of work at a new job with a new company for a public affairs manager for a Fortune 500 company. He was excited, enthused, and ready to tackle the corporate world.

One of the first people he met in the hallway on his way to his new office was the vice president of operations.

"Good morning," the newcomer greeted the executive.

The higher-ranking manager regarded him sternly. "Come into my office."

Once inside, the vice president ordered the young man to close the door, crossing behind his desk to sit without inviting the new manager to take a seat.

He said: "This is the way it works. You say 'Good morning,' and most people feel an obligation to say 'Good morning,' and pretty soon we've all said 'Good morning' and we've wasted 'X' number of man-minutes of the company's time.

"To be honest, that's just the beginning of it. After 'Good morning' you feel obligated to ask about their weekend or their families or what they watched on TV last night.

"Wasted time. So let's skip all that, shall we? I really don't care about whether or not you have a good morning. I just want you to go to work and stay at it. Understood?"

You can't blame the new employee for wondering whether he had made a bad career change.

It's never acceptable to treat work as an adult playground. But there is no sin in having fun at work.

Decades later, this same once-young manager (now in his sixties and nearing retirement) is still in the corporate world, and has made it a personal goal to find something to laugh at every single day. He tries

Having fun at work makes working ... fun.

to entertain his co-workers at appropriate times, performing what he calls his "happy dance," a convoluted mixture of the "Tigger" dance and an old soft-shoe, ball-and-chain routine.

It's funny, but it's also fun to watch him because he gets so much pleasure out of doing it.

It's okay to have fun at work, within reason, and within the boundaries of corporate policy. If work is no fun at all, then why do it?

Find something at work that will make you laugh every day. Having appropriate fun at work is as close to corporate heaven as you can get.

17 • Navel-gazing is hazardous to your health

While viewing your career future, there are four ways to focus your attention: Behind you, down, straight ahead, and up.

Except to reflect on mistakes and go over a laundry list of items learned from your experiences, there's absolutely no reason to dwell on the past. Dredging up frivolously ridiculous events that look even more so in hindsight, personal decision-making foibles, and avoidable corporate *faux pas* just wastes time and valuable mental resources.

Your time would be more wisely spent replaying what you learned and how your lessons have improved your intellectual landscape.

Looking straight ahead—maintaining the status quo—normally would not advance one's individual worth. It would instead signal professional acceptance of stagnation and eventually, degradation of position.

It's perfectly acceptable to keep one's eyes looking skyward toward loftier goals, larger and more important projects, and a title suitable to one's abilities and aspirations. But fixing your gaze in that direction has its hazards. If you don't pay attention to where you are headed, you can easily be tripped by unseen obstacles.

Looking down—navel-gazing, as it were—with excessive contemplation and unnecessary reflection on circumstances and events over which you have no control, or which don't really help your role in the company, is simply a waste of time.

The trick, then, is to keep your eye on your goals, while relying on your experience and knowledge to flash-card through available options to maximize the chance of success.

If you are going to indulge in navel-gazing, do it on your own time.

There is a major chasm between a hiccup and a certified disaster.

18 • Hiccups are no big deal

It's important for managers to learn which mistakes are important and which are mere hiccups.

A hiccup is here and gone. It is not permanent. A single hiccup does no lasting damage and few people will remember it.

A business hiccup is (for example):

- An e-mail sent without its intended attachment.
- A typographical error in a report.
- The wrong date on a document.
- Missing a minor deadline.

There are major chasms between hiccups and certified disasters. It is a frightful part of human nature that some people cannot differentiate between the two extremes. A temporarily misplaced report arouses the same reactions in some people as does an account lost to a competitor that shouldn't have been lost.

For active, multi-tasking managers, hiccups are like mosquitoes in swampy areas. They are going to pop up no matter what you do. Business hiccups, while aggravating, don't make or break careers. Those who do the hiccupping or evaluate their effect on the business may think so, however.

Swallow the hiccup by acknowledging it as a mistake, apologize if necessary, and get on to more important issues.

There will be bumps in your career path. A bump is a bump. Don't make it bigger than it is and don't allow it to ruin the journey.

19 • Great bosses don't give orders

You have arrived. You are a manager with umpteen people. Gender be damned, you are *Da Man!* Time to gear up, get your team focused on your priorities, to rise to the occasion, kick ass and take names, and whatever one hundred and thirteen other clichés you want to use. It's time to give orders and watch people scurry to do your bidding.

Whoa! Back up.

First off, Management Emperor, don't even think about giving orders. Avoid giving orders. Orders are for Third World dictators, not up-and-comers in the business world.

Great managers follow a different principle: "Give suggestions, not orders."

Here's the drill: People reporting to you are co-workers, not drones. They are your firm's most valuable resource. They are not slaves; they are the ticket to your future. Treat them like valuable commodities. Better yet, treat them like relatives you really, really like.

A great manager at his or her first departmental or project meeting would tell co-workers the following:

I don't give orders. I offer suggestions. With those suggestions you have three choices:

1) Do it, because it's the right thing to do.

2) Don't do it, but give me a better idea and a plan how you can make it work.

3) Don't do it.

Nos. 1 and 2 are always acceptable. No. 3 never is.

That sets a clear avenue for directions. It offers co-workers opportunities not only to be parts of the team, but to have input into solutions to problems or thorny projects. If you use the "suggestions, not orders"

Offering up a 'bone' occasionally is empowerment.

approach, you will empower the people you work with, acknowledge they will have good ideas, and guarantee that you will listen to them. You will lift them up, and at the same time set boundaries of protocol, punctuated by a request for their help.

Can't get much better than that.

Which brings up the inevitable question: What happens when an employee embraces the third choice—just not doing what you suggested?

Make sure your co-workers understand: "If I ever have to give you an order, that is never good for you or me— because I don't enjoy conflict."

Clear. Concise. Understandable.

The birth and growth of a great manager is not a one-event occurrence. Learning the ability to communicate will always open one of the main pathways to success.

20 • Are you a good corporate fit?

Although there are myriad trick questions in the world of business, this is not one of them: How do you fit into your vision of what the professional world should be?

Regardless of how you view, well, *you*, chances are others view you in a totally different way. They can see your strengths and they know your weaknesses.

Successful corporate leaders have the innate ability to recognize their own strengths and weaknesses, and plan their professional lives around working to maximize their strengths and minimize their weaknesses.

Too many managers believe they are total packages—everything is in place and only circumstances keep them from zooming up the corporate ladders at record paces.

You have a mental picture of the corporate world in which you want

Use your time wisely; bend your strengths to help minimize weaknesses.

to operate. But what do the corporate world and its denizens think about you?

One corporate manager—a person who has changed professions four times, and been successful with each move—readily admits he talks too much, is too loud, tends to be overbearing, can be sarcastic when trying to be humorous, and is one of the messiest managers on the planet. He talks loud, laughs louder, loves to tell long, sometimes boring stories, and is gregarious to the point of driving people away.

His desk looks like a Barbie house that was hit by a tornado. His visible organizational skills seem to be nil. Although he's labored at manipulating computer keyboards for more than 35 years, his knowledge of computers and how to make them work to enhance his productivity is on the same plateau as a circus elephant's.

But, he's successful and is considered an exceptional corporate manager by all accounts.

Without changing his Type A personality, without moving into a method of working that is totally alien to him, he has gone into every position he has held with a firm plan for success, complete dedication to company goals, and unmatched multi-tasking abilities. He exceeds company goals, and completes projects satisfactorily, under budget and on time.

Over time he has developed his own style of working within what can be a cloistered environment—the modern corporation. Here are the basic rules that have worked for this manager:

1) If someone asks for help, he stops whatever he is doing—if his present task was not requested by his immediate supervisor or the company president or CEO—and fulfills the request quickly and efficiently. This does two things: It allows the requester to start working, and allows the manager to return to his previous task. Now there are two people working, instead of one working and one waiting. The second thing it

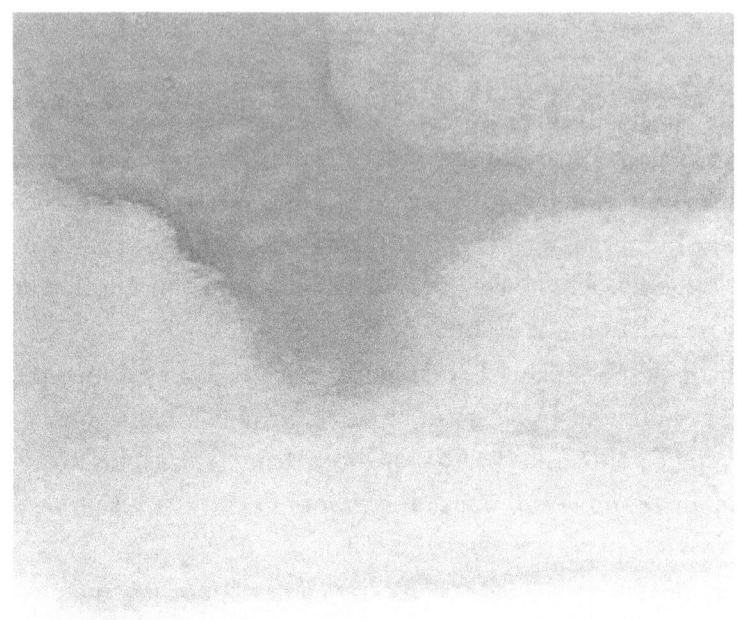

The path of success is organized by degree and design … not by sheer will.

does is put a little mark in the recipient's mind that his or her request was important enough to the manager that he stopped what he was doing to help.

2)   He sets priorities not only for himself but also for those who report to him. In fact, he requires them to set their own priorities, to be given to him as a list. When in doubt, they look at their lists, make recommendations for changes, and get the manager's sign-off. Personal involvement in deciding the direction a project should take is always preferable to a plethora of orders.

3)   He practices anticipatory management, which means providing information and support before it is requested. Few things catch upper management's attention quicker than someone who provides necessary and important information before it is requested.

4)   He's the first one to work each day and doesn't leave until a chore is finalized. He's not a workaholic, but does whatever is necessary to perform any task to the best of his ability and on the schedule important to others.

5)   He allows those reporting to him the right to make mistakes, does not chastise them for non-recurring mistakes, and encourages them to learn from their miscues.

6)   His evaluations of co-workers are fair, exacting, and pinpoint strengths as well as weaknesses. Those evaluations are followed up by objectives designed to minimize or eliminate problem areas in personality and/or work habits.

7)   Like all competent managers, he doesn't seek to place blame when something goes awry. Rather, he looks for the glitches in the systems used, and eliminates opportunities to repeat mistakes.

8)   He considers overlong contemplation of a problem as a major deterrent to positive action. He looks at facts, reviews structure or protocol, relies on his experience, asks for input from others, listens to

In true life and business teams, the hard work is always shared.

recommendations—and makes a decision. During the planning process, he encourages co-workers to identify problem areas and discuss possible scenarios to minimize damage.

9) Nothing is more important than a request from his boss or a corporate executive. Face time, and/or personal requests for his services take top priority. Period.

10) He rates himself on every finished project on a scale from 1 to 10. He analyzes each project upon completion and tries to ferret out what he could have done better, and then remembers the lessons he learned. He considers a consistent grade of "8" or higher as acceptable.

Could this manager curb his natural tendencies, tone down his personality quirks, move a little more to the right of Type A to, maybe, a Type A-minus? Of course, he could. But obviously he has not, for several reasons, the most valid of which is that he has succeeded in spite of certain quirks normally assumed to be quasi-aberrant in the business world.

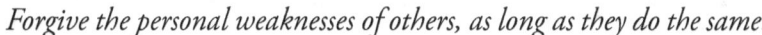

Forgive the personal weaknesses of others, as long as they do the same.

Ride a wind stream that's comfortable, not one that's merely expedient.

21 • Don't 'get out of the box'!

popular theme among coaches of would-be managers on how to progress in the global economy is to tell them to "get out of the box!"

On the count of three, let's take that catchphrase and throw it in the corporate trash bin of clichés.

In many cases, boxes are good. They are built from a company's traditions and values, from a strong mission statement that emphasizes service over self, and from the sweat and dedication of generations of good, dedicated, hard workers who believed in their product or service.

So boxes can be good. But change is inevitable. How do these seemingly conflicting corporate axioms "make nice" in today's fast-moving business world?

Changing is . . . emerging in a different form.

54

It's not so much a necessity to "get out of the box," as it is to define the box's parameters and then, as needs and opportunities dictate, expand your own business "box."

People who have no boxes to begin with can be scary to co-workers, supervisors and upper-level management. Unbridled enthusiasm for new projects not connected to core competencies, or a cornucopia of abstract ideas thrown helter-skelter across the corporate landscape can be mistaken for a lack of respect for the company's caretakers and the goals they pursue.

There's a large difference between, for example, a "change merchant" and an "off-the-wall nut case."

Don't confuse the two, or believe that both paths will end up at the same place.

22 • Learn the art of 'unthinking'

If you think you are ready to take the corporate world by storm, if you think you are ready for the challenges ahead, if you think you can run a department or even the company better than whoever else is in charge, think again.

Better yet, "unthink" yourself.

Great managers take time out on occasion to evaluate their lives, careers, decisions, and processes. They look for changes that need to be made so they can continue on their paths to be the best they can be.

If you are not changing, you are either stagnating or regressing. Those are the only choices.

You cannot progress without self-analysis and making changes where necessary, or taking a route you may find more mentally comfortable, which would be to accept advice from those whom you trust and are willing to give you an honest critique. In either case, what you take away from the exercise is up to you.

Unthinking is difficult, at best. It involves separating your comfortable self from what you know and use every day in your professional life—time management, multi-tasking procedures, human resources issues, protocols for accomplishing tasks, and on and on.

In mastering the art of unthinking, you have to question what you do and how and why you do it the way you do. You have to think about how you view yourself, then *unthink* those thoughts before *rethinking* and reconstructing a brand new view of what you want to be in the future. In other words, you tear down and reconstruct your *Circumference of Me* into a reorganized, yet recognizable and functional format.

You may find that in unthinking yourself, many of the managerial traits you now possess are absolutely perfect for getting to the next point along your career path.

More than likely, however, you will be surprised how many procedures you take for granted will need tweaking in order to make you more responsive, productive, efficient, and more of a team player.

The ability to unthink one's self—to objectively tear yourself down and build a new model—is like having an emergency first aid kit in the trunk of your car: You don't realize its value until you truly need it.

Floating new ideas should be considered an adventure.

23 • Float those ideas

In the world of business, there are few things more depressing than a deflated idea that once held promise.

In companies, associations, educational institutions and groups, many more good ideas find their way into the mental gutters of obscurity than ever are pursued and given life.

You have ideas, some good, some bad. Some are so horrible they emit a psychic stench.

Learning to differentiate between good ideas, not-fully-formed ideas with promise, and ideas that need to be buried in concrete—twice!—is part of the growth cycle of leaders. The sifting process is not clear-cut; there is no self-help recipe for success.

Differences among ideas, personalities of people who project the ideas, times and circumstances dictate whether an idea has merit.

Regardless, the good ideas may lie dormant alongside the stinkers unless you have the confidence to push them out of the mental hatchery and see if they can stand, nay, *fly*, on their merits.

When you float an idea, make sure it has a strong tether; even floating ideas need to be grounded in reality.

The foggiest of notions can only become clear when released.

24 • Bottle the fog

Regardless of position, problem, or project, there will come a time when fog rolls in—not on little cat feet, but stomping, in boots bearing razor-sharp cleats.

Fighting various degrees of infernal fog—i.e., cloudy goals or obscure directions to reach the goals—is part of life in the management world. Any set of circumstances that obscure the mission, process, protocol, or projected end results can be a project-threatening fog bank. It is an obstruction that must be dealt with quickly and efficiently if there is to be any chance of success.

People, places, unseen events, unknown terrors, personality clashes, bashing egos—all have the potential to stir up blinding fog that obscures the reality of what could be, by creating a false, diluted picture of what should never be.

There are uses for fog, assuredly. Bottle it in your mind. And pull it out during boring meetings, to release in little snake-tendrils, and will it to diffuse the bad ideas that inevitably arise in catch-as-catch-can managers' free-for-alls.

Use your fog wisely—not to deter the ideas just because you don't like the initial concepts, or just because you can. Learn when to keep the stopper on tight and when to release the fog to refocus the creative process.

Fog: Use it for good, not evil.

25 • Be the impossible

Whatever anyone claims, there are only two things that are, truly, impossible: 1) Leave this world alive, and 2) Strike a wet match on a wet cake of soap.

Everything else is possible. If you think it, you can do it; if you dream it, you can plan, design, study, and work to create pathways to make it a reality.

People who believe a seemingly impossible task is exactly that are exactly right for their own, wrong reasons. "Impossible" is more of a mindset than an actuality. There are too many examples of people accomplishing tasks once thought impossible to give much serious consideration to such a flawed premise.

Believing the impossible is possible is the first step to accomplishing something truly wonderful. *Knowing* the impossible is possible is

The list of things truly impossible is quite short.

Not possible! Yeah, right! (Proving two positives do not necessarily make a negative.)

the second and final step to success. To reach that lofty mental peak, which few ever attempt to climb for fear of ridicule or failure, you not only must believe the impossible can be accomplished, but you must change your own mental and/or physical boundaries. By utilizing your new attributes, your new strengths, that come through your discovery of the *Circumference of Me*, you can become a force who knows no boundaries, who will not accept the notion that tradition or circumstances dictate the ultimate outcome of a project, or whether it is viable.

Look outside yourself. Expand your personal circumference to accept accomplishing what others consider impossible as a normal part of your personal and professional life.

If you want to do the impossible, be the impossible.

26 • Pursue the passionate struggle

No one said life is fair, and if they did, they lied. Life is not always fair; it's only life.

Same holds true for a career path.

First things first. And the first thing is a stern reality check. Many fast-track managers (especially ones who are fast-tracked only in their minds) need to put aside all the motivational hoopla and shrill nonsense that starts with, "If you can dream it," and ends with, "you can do it!"

Circumstances sometimes dictate that regardless of your dreams, your goals, your attributes, your career plan, your internal and external support structure, your experience, and your will to win, you are sometimes going to come up short.

Your dreams need to keep pace with the realities that are you. They need to be part of you in an intrinsic, personal sense, in your "Circumstance of Me." Your dreams need to be expansive, but obtainable, based on current realities. Still, you should always summon dreams that may not be realities for today. Those dreams fuel your will to succeed beyond your present personal and professional limits.

It is not true, regardless of what other management or motivational books or $5,000-an-appearance speakers may tell you, that you are the lone key to your personal success. It *is* true that your chances of finding someone who will believe in you for yourself are as remote as finding a four-carat diamond in a Happy Meal.

Sheer faith in your abilities won't bring you the Golden Ring of Success, or help you understand The Psychology of Human Motivation, or give you the ability to grasp The Universal Principles of Personal Achievement, or guide you to learn Where Achievement and Fulfillment Meet.

You cannot measure personal success by drips, drabs, and drops that refuse to commingle with the reality of your *Circumference of Me.* Your

Rise above the fray. Enjoy the view.

success will come—or won't—along a reality river of circumstances, some reasonably planned, others random. What winners strive for is to build a bridge that rises above corporate pettiness and the messy brouhaha of territorial fighting that rages in virtually every company.

If you can energize yourself by listening to a corps of motivational speakers—Zig Ziglar, Kenneth Blanchard, Napoleon Hill, Denis Waitley or Brian Tracey—then, more power to you. If reading every new book on personal motivation and keys to success in business helps, then, by all means, buy books and author lecture tickets.

But, in the end, you are only picking up tidbits that might help you go around, over, under, or through the bogs of one's personal battlefields. No motivational program or communications tool—not even this book—holds a magic elixir to change lives. That can only be accomplished through understanding and committing to expanding the *Circumference of Me*.

Your army is, indeed, of one soldier. You and only you can make the necessary decisions that can change your life to fit your dreams and goals.

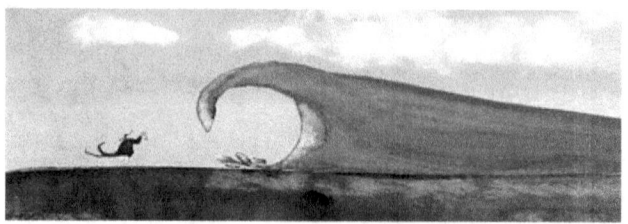

Stand fast. And charge whatever frightens you.

27 • Charging the ROAR!

On the Serengeti plans of Africa, lions hunt antelope. The prey are swift of foot; the hunters are not as fast. Regardless, lions have to eat. Presented with an age-old problem, the lions figured out how to change the way the game is played.

The old males lie still in the tall grass. The younger members of the pride, mostly females, stalk the antelope herd, nudging it toward the grass, and the old lions.

As if attached to a mental string, the stalking lions charge as a group, and the antelopes sprint away crazy-fast until they get close to the hidden males. All the old lions have to do is stand up and ROAR! The single act terrifies the herd into reversing direction—straight into the ready claws and teeth of the pride.

The lions act on instinct, as do their prey. If the antelope could overcome their instinctive fear and charge the ROAR, they would break through untouched.

Their hesitation and their fear are their undoing.

Charge the ROAR in your life. Recognize your fear for what it is and work to overcome it. You will find yourself in the open; you will be free. That's when you catch your breath and learn how to smile again.

Processed
Advice

28 • Aaaagh! Be a warrior!

Any way you look at it, the corporate tribe is divided into three distinct groups of workers: Chiefs, warriors, support staff.

Normally, chiefs attain their positions in a company by working up through the ranks—if not at the present company, then at some other. The warriors protect the company, its brand and its franchise in the marketplace. Support staff members are the linchpin of a company's success, day in and day out, and their accomplishments and assistance should never be forgotten. From their ranks will come future warriors and chiefs.

The chiefs make policies, establish goals, give project overviews, and assign critical management tasks and projects they believe will mean success for the company.

The warriors carry out the policies, set up steps to achieve the chiefs' goals in a reasonable and efficient manner, control expenses, and teach support staff how to grow as individuals and increase their value to the company, thereby enhancing the company's wealth in human resources.

The warriors carry the company's spears and shields. As the first line of both offense and defense, they battle competitors daily, conduct reconnaissance to search for weaknesses, and ferret out opportunities. Their job is to present the most powerful, positive image of the company possible.

Be wary and cautious at times ... but never afraid.

As a warrior, your future and the future of your company make the tip of your spear.

You are a warrior, and your future, and the future of your company, is the tip of your spear.

You are the beginning, and the end, of a corporation's success. Without you, without your efforts, without your determination, drive, work ethic, creativity, attention to detail, and ability to create order from chaos, the company would not be as successful as it could be.

Do you believe that about your company, about yourself?

Great!

Then, what are you waiting for?

Stop standing around looking at the battlefield. Grab your spear and get to work!

It is from the support staff ranks that future leaders will emerge. In this cocoon stage of corporate development, the norm is to think creative thoughts that could positively change the company, but not to voice them for fear of ridicule. At this time, the strongest players should be learning a valuable lesson: which manager style to emulate, and which to avoid.

It is a time of personal discovery, of figuring out what boundaries are considered normal and how to expand those boundaries, to enhance your potential in the workplace.

It's a time to look, listen, and learn. The process is not unlike the growing-up process of a lion cub. It takes a cub more than two years to learn how to be independent, how to recognize opportunities, and how to take advantage of them.

Be patient at this stage of professional development. If, unlike the lion cub, you leave the protection of "family" too soon, you may jeopardize your future.

Embrace the ideas of others ... and respect those who present them.

29 • Shhhhhhhhhh!

There are many business tenets followed by successful leaders of major corporations. None, however, are more important than the ones expressed in three little words:

1) Listen.

2) Learn.

3) Listen.

Good managers know when to talk and what to say. Great managers know when to talk and when to listen—and work hard not to get the two mixed up.

There are distinct steps to being a great communicator, and one of the most important is not to talk, but to listen. Not only does listening open up the possibility of two-way communication, it gives the speaker a sense of self-worth through your acknowledgment that his or her opinion is important.

But it's not enough simply to listen. To be meaningful, the message has to be acknowledged and then run through a manager's mental colander so vital information can be extracted—information that could mean the difference between success or failure. Analysis is a natural part of obtaining information. Just as managers (and all other corporate workers) should learn to listen, whoever imparts information must make sure that the information being bartered—in exchange for recognition, praise, or fluffy mental hugs—is full of pith, i.e., substance.

While it is perfectly acceptable—not to mention expected—for managers to give feedback in return for information received, it is important to revert back to Step 1.

After initial information is offered, and a response is made, further comments should be requested. It's time, once again, to listen.

A manager's comment might trigger additional thoughts that will

Regardless of status in life, in business it's important to sing the same tune.

roll out during the second phase of communication. These comments may be even more valuable than the original information, because they have not been rehearsed. They are coming from virgin territory, unencumbered by self-censorship and corporate decorum.

Listen, learn, and listen.

Search for the pith on both ends of the communications spectrum. Learn to dish it out and recognize it when you get it.

30 • Texting while juggling over a pit of alligators

There is no secret to the power you can achieve if you are above average at multi-tasking.

Let's start with a truism: It is difficult to do more than two things at one time—not impossible, just extremely difficult, and hard for non-multi-taskers to imagine.

While there is a constant need for single-task-oriented workers in practically any company or non-profit group, people who want to rise above their professional-world rearing need to add the Multi-Tasking Tool to their business repertoires.

Multi-tasking would be quite simple if there were no time limits on individual tasks. It would be easy if you could but work on one task for a time until you hit a blank spot, then switch to Chore 2 until lunchtime. In the afternoon, in between your regular break and e-mail checks, you spend an hour each on Chore 3 and Chore 4.

Unfortunately, that's not multi-tasking. That's Chore Stacking.

Multi-tasking is the ability to start a project or task, jump to an-

Sometimes work can be a struggle. Advice: Suck it up!

other that pops up with a higher priority level, slip in a few e-mails to keep other people informed, check out a request that popped up a week ago—which you performed and reported on—to see if it was received, add a third project that calls for a quick turnaround—and do all that by the end of the work day.

Multi-tasking is not just starting myriad tasks, it's bringing all of them to satisfactory conclusions, on time and under budget.

The inherent problem with multi-tasking at a breakneck rate is crack-dropping. There is always a danger of some project, some request, falling through the mental cracks. Learning how to manage projects—keeping them in some semblance of order, and drawing up a firm, prioritized to-do list when you feel overwhelmed—is a key step up the corporate ladder.

Sometimes too many tasks will end up in your in-basket and there won't be time to accomplish them. What to do?

It's the same situation a waiter or waitress must deal with in a restaurant short on wait staff. The solution: Acknowledge the problem head-on. Experienced wait staff tell customers up front whether there

Successful managers rise above expectations by adding tools to their arsenals.

Ladder climbing does not come without possible slip-ups.

could be a problem with service; they constantly acknowledge customers with looks and nods from across the room; they check on the customers as often as possible.

They are playing a customer-relations game that emphatically states: "I'm doing the best I can and I will be with you directly."

The same holds true for any manager who tries to do too much in too little time. Your solution: Acknowledge the problem with your supervisor, ask for assistance in setting priorities, and work to set up realistic deadlines.

If a chore is not completed, it's never because of time, it's because of the ranking of priorities.

31 • Three unspoken wishes

This chapter has absolutely nothing to do with how to position yourself to be a great manager and leader.

It does, however, have everything to do with being happy. Being happy in what you do will positively affect your performance as a manager and leader.

Remember when you were a kid and had dreams and aspirations? One executive of a non-profit organization confessed that as a teenager he made a list of a hundred things he wanted to do during his lifetime. Over time, he has accomplished more than sixty of those original goals, and several more are within his grasp.

Many sounded simple: Visit all fifty states; swim in the Atlantic and Pacific Oceans; raft a wild river in Central America; drive the Autobahn at top speed; see a bear in the wild; hike the Grand Canyon; relax along a snow-fed stream in the Alps.

The dreams of the child became the realities of the man. At this writing he has reached all those goals, with the exception of visiting all fifty states. He has visited forty-seven, but there is no doubt he will hit all fifty within the next few years.

He is goal-oriented, and goal-oriented people are driven by the best of all motivational factors: personal satisfaction.

Some of his early goals—go down the Amazon River, climb Mount Kilimanjaro, walk along the Great Wall of China, photograph head-

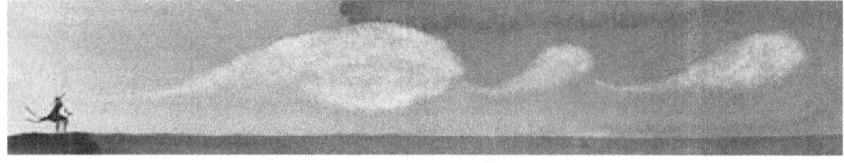

Wishes, even those unspoken, can direct life's journey.

Make a wish . . . or three.

hunters in Borneo—may not be realized. But, honestly, it doesn't matter. The fact that he set goals and met many of them over his lifetime is what counts.

If you don't have personal goals, make a list. Write them down. Revisit the list from time to time and adjust the goals as you experience life changes.

At the very least, think about giving yourself three unspoken goals. They are your goals. They are personal. Hold them close and repeat this mantra:

Make three goals. Nurture them. Reach them.

It's not a childish exercise. It's a key to having a balanced life.

Dream the dreams others wished they had dreamed. Create realities from dreams where others fail to do so.

32 • Management or leadership

Captain Grace Hopper, the oldest commissioned officer in the Navy in 2009, believed there are contrasting and conflicting natures of management and leadership. She has a point.

Regardless of military rank, you cannot manage men in battle. You have to *lead* them.

This is a professional bugaboo, because learning to be a leader is one of the most difficult chores imaginable. And the job is even more difficult when you consider that managers love managers, but the rank and file love leaders.

Confusing? Sure. But it's true.

Let's break it down: Leaders can be disconcerting. They don't fit in a conventional mold. They are doers, not merely thinkers. They are un-

A leader shows how thorny problems and seemingly impossible tasks can be subdued.

Leaders carry the banner, a sign of respect for the troops.

predictable, and full of surprises. All those traits cause anxiety among many mainline managers. Leaders possess both common sense and creativity, an uncommon combination of managerial traits, for sure. It's the same combination that throws up the red flags of schizophrenia on the Briggs-Meyer psychological test.

Left brain! Right brain! Which one? Both?!?! Oh, my God!

History is resplendent with stories of leaders. Alexander the Great ate, slept, and suffered with his men, and often was the first in line during an attack. General George Patton was despised by certain higher-ups, but loved by the men he commanded because he believed in equality at all levels of service. He boasted time and again that he and his men could do the impossible, then he made it happen.

On the other hand, most managers are safe, conservative in thought and action, predictable to the point of boredom, and conform to organizational structures even when they prohibit free thought and positive action.

Sometimes a leader can make a permanent impression through a small gesture. A conservative Fortune 500 company once had a strict dress code in the corporate office: suits and ties for men, dresses (with hose) for women.

Shortly after a new president was named, the employees were informed each Friday would be business casual. Soon after, the business casual policy was extended to every day.

That new corporate president was an exceptional manager, but he quickly established himself as more than that. He was a true leader with an employee base that would do whatever it took to make sure he succeeded in his new role. He understood that while a dressed-up workforce might look really good, a comfortable workforce would be happier and more productive.

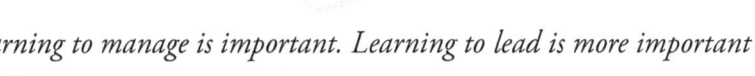

Learning to manage is important. Learning to lead is more important than that.

33 • Face the facts

A t some point in a worker's career, he or she will be managed by a manager who can't manage. It is a fact of the world of business.

What are the warning signs of bad managers?

1) They give orders.

2) They expect the orders to be carried out, no exceptions and no freelancing, even if a slight change could produce more positive results.

3) They don't request or want ideas that differ from their own. They didn't think of them, so they can't be good.

4) They enjoy the attention of brown-nosers and gobble up praise like an Oreck vacuum cleaner.

5) They recognize and fear competence, innate talent, and intelligence in other workers. They will do whatever they can to squash them, because they make them feel threatened.

6) They like their little slices of the corporate world just the way they are, and don't abide any attempts to change them.

7) They are blind and deaf to any efforts to correct errant paths or create new opportunities for the company.

Attacking the problem of a bad manager head-on usually is not an option. Many companies protect such managers. Clout and tenure still count in the corporate environment.

So, what do you do?

Perform your duties in exacting detail, finish every assigned task on time, assist co-workers at every opportunity (Who knows who will be in charge of what in the future?), and look outside your immediate department or organization for opportunities to do other work that can get you noticed in a positive light.

It is ironic, in a way, that many great leaders will admit they learned as much from so-called "bad" managers as from managers they admired. It can be a life lesson to work for a bad manager and compile a list of "what not to do."

If you are confident in your abilities, it's important to keep your feet on the ground while your eyes scan beyond the horizon, looking for opportunities. And it does no harm occasionally to think that one day, that bad, low-level manager will still be a bad, low-level manager while you will be a leader in a much more important role.

Great managers create an environment for change so poor performers can improve. Those managers are recognized for their efforts to take the time to make others better.

34 • Danger, Will Robinson!

Progressive businesses need risk-takers. They need managers who encourage up-and-comers to take risks. Great managers realize mistakes will happen as a result, but that the rewards will be worth the risks, and that competent managers will emerge from such constructive exercises of personal freedom.

It's simple to take chances. Just do something that hasn't been done before. What's difficult is learning to look at every opportunity from a variety of angles, to figure out the best path with the largest possible reward, and to build a step-by-step game plan to ensure success.

It's extremely important for managers to be able to recognize potential danger signals early in the process. The robot who warned the youngest of the "Lost in Space" clan in the early days of television, "Danger, Will Robinson!" had the ability to recognize peril. That, and knowing how to take action to minimize damage, are valuable attributes.

Figure out the best path for you … and stick with it.

Recognizing the target keeps personal focus where it can do the most good.

A chaotic, shotgun approach toward possibly dangerous projects is a guaranteed way to find yourself in the unemployment line. You can check out the target with shotgun sights, but in the end, the approach of a good manager is more like a sniper with a rifle.

The rifle approach entails careful planning and preparation, a solid line-up on a discernible and reachable goal, an unerring ability not only to find the target, but to figure out the best path to hit it, to take careful aim, and to be able to pull the trigger at the right moment.

The ability to see a broad landscape of opportunity, then narrowly define and focus efforts on realistic programs and services before the competition even knows there's a target market, maximizes upside for your company and makes you more valuable to your organization.

Recognizing danger in a corporate environment is difficult. Those employees who can do so and have the courage to speak out not only enhance their personal worth, but that of the company as well.

Getting caught in the policy trap endangers the viability of business entities.

35 • Those dumb policies

Nothing frustrates competent managers, distributors and customers like policies that were approved unilaterally because of specific problems, with no thought of possible exceptions and no timely review to see if the policies stay valid.

A customer walks into a sports store looking for a good pair of walking shoes to wear on a trip he's about to take. He has money in his pocket and is ready to spend it. The only other people in the store are a clerk and a manager.

The customer finds shoes he wants to try, and the clerk fetches a pair in his size. He also hands the customer a pair of footies.

"I don't want to use the footies," the customer says. "I want to try them on with thicker socks, like the ones I will be wearing on my trip."

"We don't do that," the clerk responds flatly.

The customer looks at a nearby rack of sports socks. "You don't sell sports socks?"

"No, we sell them, but you can't try them on in the store."

"But I'm going to buy them."

"You can't try them on in the store. It's company policy."

At the customer's insistence, the manager is summoned.

"It's company policy," the manager says. "Can't try socks on in the store."

"Can I go to the cash register with the socks, pay for them, then put them on, and try on the shoes?"

"No trying on socks in the store. It's policy."

Now the customer is having fun. "Can I buy the socks, go to my car, put on the socks, come back in the store and try on the shoes?"

"Yes. That would be fine."

In this case, the customer takes his money and goes elsewhere to buy shoes.

A policy is only good for the unique situation for which it was introduced, and should only apply to that situation. Policies, like just about anything else connected to business, need to be reviewed on a regular basis, and changed as situations warrant.

Employees on the front lines should have the leeway to make decisions that make customers happy and the company money.

Policies to avoid business chaos are important. Dumb policies are ... just dumb.

When riding the winds of change, look for the strongest currents.

36 • Learn how to make change

The corporate graveyard is filled with businesses that were, in their primes, the best at what they did. Yet they failed. Number Ones became Number Nones.

The obituaries tell the tales, always with the same read-between-the-lines line: "Faced with changes in the market, the company refused to *change* and adapt to new realities."

"Change." The specter of change is the Scary Clown among all eventualities a company and its managers must face. Routine, familiar policies and procedures, and traditional protocols, even for how decisions are made, are security blankets for a brain-dead organization.

That's why the world has created a class of helper known as The Consultant. Consultants are outside experts brought inside a company to allow the possibility of change to be explored without damaging the reputations or fragile egos of company insiders.

Regardless of where ideas or change originate, there always will be the Purveyors of the Anti-Change Philosophy. You know the type: "It

Advocating change can be a lonely position within a business.

was good enough back in The Day, so it's good enough now."

That inane argument is heard in Boardroomdoms around the world, and backed up by such statements as:

"We don't want to act hastily. That policy has been in place a long time."

"I remember the last big change we went through. Bad—very, very bad."

"The company is doing fine. Why are we wanting to change what's not broken?"

"Change! What's it good for? Absolutely nothing!"

What every corporation needs, but few have, are change merchants. But most organizations don't encourage in-house change merchants, and usually tolerate them only in the upper levels. Change merchants are rare; change merchants who really can make change happen are rarer still within the confines of Corporate U.

What does a change merchant look like? He or she looks like the average employee, but with a backbone and guts. Change merchants don't advocate change for change's sake, but because they are convinced that if the market environment is constantly changing, then it makes good business sense to change with it, or to change before the next big consumer wave hits.

Floating ideas: The tool of choice for change merchants.

Change is inevitable in any company. It's like stock fluctuations, the air conditioning breaking down on the hottest day of the year, a broken shoelace when there's no time to fix it, or PowerPoint freezing up in the middle of an important presentation.

Change is the driving force that opens up new avenues of opportunity for the company and its employees. It's important, it's healthy for a company and its workers, and it's going to happen whether you like it or not. If you can't be a leader for change, at least be a willing spectator. Being against change of any kind doesn't mark you as a traditionalist; it marks you as a corporate Neanderthal.

Those who defy change will not be around to see it.

Consultants can provide necessary building blocks to instigate change.

37 • Fighting is a part of corporate life

Of course, they shouldn't, but people being people, they will get into fights in your corporate environment.

Avoid fights—figuratively and literally—whenever possible. But if you have to fight, then, as in any battle, there's a time to plan, a time to retreat, and a time to attack.

What is worth fighting for within your work environment? The Top 3 contenders are:

1) Job,
2) Credibility,
3) Ideas.

Fight for your job. If you like your job, fight to keep it. Stake your corporate claim and fight by being the best you can be at every single task, doing what is asked and asking for more, anticipating the needs of your supervisor and co-workers and delivering exemplary work, increasing your corporate worth by increasing your knowledge in all possible areas, and looking for opportunities to perform unassigned tasks to make your boss look good to his or her boss.

Fight for your credibility, which is the equivalent of corporate capital. A credible worker is always asked to perform essential tasks because he or she has succeeded time and time again on other assigned tasks. Perform above expectations, and outstanding credibility grades or reviews will follow.

What is worth fighting for in your world?

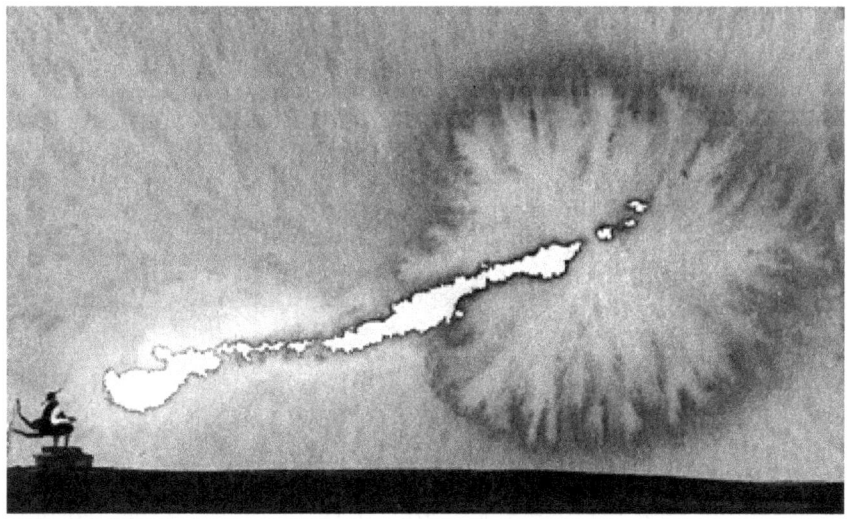

When you have an idea founded in personal belief or experience, speak up.

Fight for your ideas. It is amazing that so many ideas to increase a company's revenues or save millions are never implemented because the words, the plans, are never presented. Those ideas lay fallow in the minds of workers and mid-level managers, either because they are not encouraged to provide vital information up the executive chain of command or they are too fearful for their jobs to speak out.

Who is in the best position to know when a company is spending money it doesn't have to spend, or is missing sales because of a missing cog in the product machine—the person who sees that situation every day, or a manager three rungs removed from the action?

Speak up when it benefits the company. In good businesses, educational institutions or associations, someone will listen.

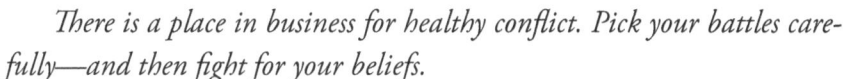

There is a place in business for healthy conflict. Pick your battles carefully—and then fight for your beliefs.

38 • When projects go toes-up

A business wants to accomplish something. It has a project. You are the team leader or a valued team member. You have a starting point, a definitive goal, and an action plan.

Everything is going great … then something goes wrong, and all of a sudden, the straight line to success looks like a Rocky Mountain switchback trail.

First things first: You do whatever it takes to get the project back on track, on schedule and as close to budget as possible. You keep notes on corrective actions you took, for future reference.

You and your team are good. You finish the job and the lightning strike that disrupted the work flow is a memory, a blip on the corporate radar.

So, on to the next project, right?

Nope. Not yet. Not even close.

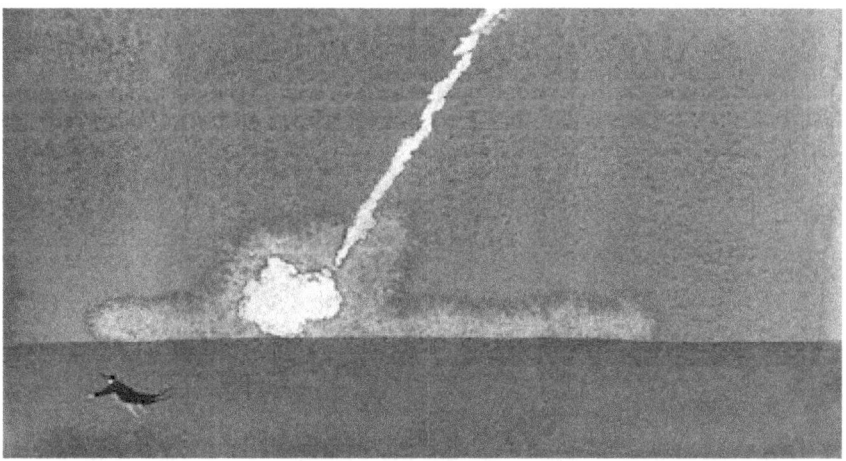

When problems derail a project, don't run and hide—get the project back on track.

Anytime an aberration causes the near-swamping of a project or chore, it's important to realize there was an aberration. Finding it is the key to preventing a future occurrence. But most important is learning what caused the aberration in the first place.

Going all the way back to the beginning of the project and retracing steps to the point the problem appeared should uncover the cause. Knowing the cause will help you change internal systems and protocols so you can be sure that particular problem will not sidetrack a future project.

An aberration simply is an external influence that caused a change in the expected pathway to success. Finding it and understanding how and why it happened will lessen the chances it will happen again.

Life lessons should be learned not just by studying successful cases. They can also be learned by studying what caused failures among important projects and companies.

39 • Outward-looking-in is A-OK

Not a single company in the world has had sustained growth for many years without managers who are different. Most managers embrace the status quo. They believe tradition is more important than innovation. They don't take risks, are the corporate equivalent of the cartoon ostrich (head stuck in the sand), strive to be yes-men to executives, and actively subdue creative thought in themselves and others.

It is the out-of-the-mold managers, those around-the-corner thinkers, who propel a company forward, who give it life, create an atmosphere of success, and who supervise positive change.

It is the outward-looking-in managers who run companies and look for others like themselves to work by their sides.

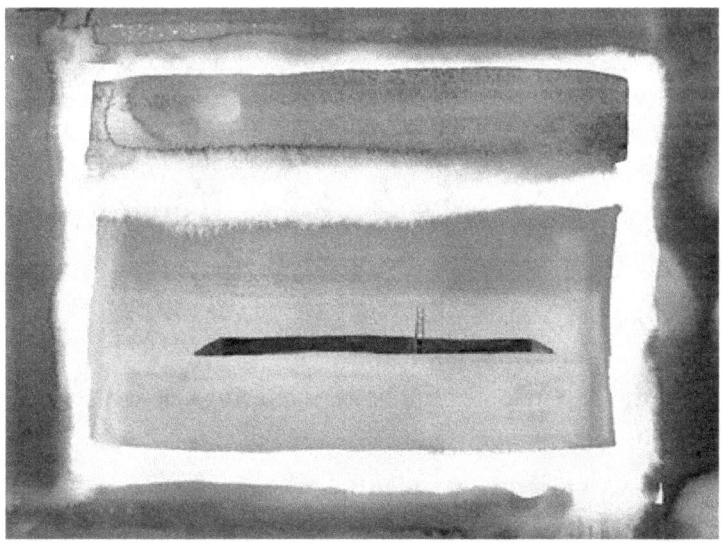

How did you get in a hole? How can you extricate yourself?

40 • Anticipate problems

Problems are a major part of life in the corporate world. A primary job for most managers is to manage problems.

Good managers try to handle problems as they pop up. Great managers have a knack for seeing problems before they happen, then acting to minimize or prevent fallout. Whether they rely on experience or use common sense and logic, or both, they anticipate the sizes and shapes of problems. They know what kind of damage they can do. They know problems never go away and must be managed appropriately or they will return, bigger and badder and with twice as many teeth and claws.

It's a harsh reality of business that while you can manage to handle a fair share of problems, others have the potential to crush your spirit.

Don't try to be a hero, fixing every problem that raises its gnarly

Problems have solutions. You just have to find them.

head. Even the best manager can be on the losing side when faced with wrestling a problem bearing a multitude of thorns.

The five steps of problem-solving are:

1) Recognize the problem as a problem.

2) Analyze its potential for destruction.

3) Decide on a course of action that will benefit the company and kill or maim the smallest number of your co-workers.

4) Take action.

And, finally (on particularly nasty problems that you don't solve on the first try):

5) Regroup, re-analyze, use your imagination to select another, more innovative course of action, and attack again. Repeat this step as many times as necessary.

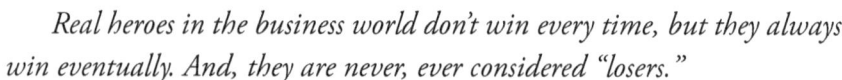

Real heroes in the business world don't win every time, but they always win eventually. And, they are never, ever considered "losers."

41 • 'CYA' means ~ ah, you know!

Learning to "cover your ass" is an integral lesson in becoming a manager. "CYA" is not a negative expression, but a positive one, if you look at it in the right way.

"CYA" simply means doing your job and documenting it. It does not mean you should create documents that keep you from looking bad. There are times when, no matter what you do, you are going to look bad. You can't make decisions, multi-task six simultaneous projects, plan, strategize, create presentations and slice, dice, and julienne without making a mistake here or there.

When you make that mistake, don't CYA *post mortem*. Take a giant leap and confess. Take the blame and the heat that might (make that "usually will") come along with it.

Saying, "My bad, and I learned a valuable lesson from the experience" wins points and avoids long-term demerits.

Take a giant leap and understand confession is good for the soul—and career.

There are advantages to taking action against the normal protocol.

42 • Trekking in the wilderness

Today, the Road Less Traveled has become a wilderness. Our business paths and patterns have become so disrupted we have been forced off the usual roadways to success.

Taking a chance on a seldom-used path is unfamiliar, scary, and risky at its worst. At its best, it stands you apart from the herd and opens up new vistas to explore.

Wisdom is gained by managers who stray from prescribed and well-worn paths. Wandering opens up new vistas, horizons of heretofore unseen challenges and opportunities, and provides a different perspective from the normal routine, allowing clear and previously unimagined solutions to problems once considered unsolvable.

Allowing time and making the commitment to leave traditional pathways of business in search of new beginnings and endings creates an environment conducive to surprises of volcanic proportions. Resolve to see challenges in different perspectives; view the unseen forces of the future as your own personal security blanket, not as nebulous will-o'-the-wisps that haunt your dreams.

Many workers go through life wearing self-applied blinders. Opportunities come readily to the ones who keep their eyes open and wits at the ready.

Change can be encouraged by outside influences; true change must come from within.

Improve your mental dexterity by exploring new ways to accomplish tasks.

43 • Be mentally ambidextrous

As you progress in your chosen profession, you will face various ways to take advantage of opportunities or solve problems. Those options will run the gamut from crystal-clear to myopic and blurry.

It takes time, energy and dedication to know a true opportunity or a real problem when you see it, then figure out what to do about it. At the same time, you have to decide what part of your experience, what advice you have picked up along your journey, or what chapter in *Circumference of Me* to pull out and mold to your needs.

It is not enough to think you are good enough to solve a problem or take advantage of an opportunity all by yourself. You have to have confidence to believe you *know* the right approach to guarantee success. To do that, you have to be able to quickly analyze all sides of a situation and decide on which path to take to create an environment for success.

You must develop an instinct to know how a problem or opportunity can best be solved or exploited. You do that by developing the ability to work equally well as a lone striker or as part of a cohesive unit.

You don't have to pick one or the other. The most successful managers have learned how to be one and the other.

Leaders sometimes stand alone. The best leaders often journey into the valleys.

44 • Four tiny words

The path of a leader can be very lonely, indeed. Toting a heavy load, especially for the long haul, never has been, is not, nor ever will be a one-person job.

The four hardest words for a person in charge of any project are the same four words that co-workers with an ounce of company pride or professional attitude love to hear: *I need your help.*

In which category do you fall? (Pick one).

1) Bad manager
2) Mediocre manager
3) Good manager
4) Great manager

The four words, "I need your help," are never included in any pronouncement by managers who fall into the bad and mediocre categories. To those graduates of Neanderthal U. (with a B.S. degree in B.S.

Ask for help when you need it ... every time. It's a sign of strength.

and a GPA of 2.4 on a 4.0 scale), "I need your help" is as foreign as Farsi.

The phrase "I need your help" is not, as some managers believe, an admission of weakness. It is a simple phrase that contains in its thirteen letters one of the most important management tools. No manager is infallible, and admitting when you need help is a statement of confidence: *I know when to ask for assistance. I would rather ask for help than fail in my mission.*

Great managers (and good managers who strive to be great) not only ask for help when they need it, but also ask for help when they don't.

Asking for help is a sincere form of flattery, and a great motivational tool for up-and-comers. It can also be useful for employees you believe may feel left out and need a recognition boost.

"I need your help." It costs nothing but the time to speak the words.

45 • Another four words to know

Did that last chapter say that those four tiny words were the hardest words for a manager to utter?

Well, that is not exactly true.

The real four hardest words to insert into a manager's vocabulary are much harder and a lot less popular.

There are managers in every company—you know them, observe them, work for them, and perhaps you are even one of them—who deny the existence of simple facts. They see nothing wrong with being deceitful, exaggerating, embellishing, misrepresenting, telling whoppers, blackening up white lies, displaying mendacity, engaging in extreme hyperbole, performing snow jobs, weaving fables, prevaricating the heck out of tales, and just plain lying to cover up when they mess up.

Why? Why go to all that trouble? Getting away with lying to escape blame for a foul-up means you lied and didn't get caught. Getting caught means you lied and aren't very good at it.

Mistakes happen. Learn from them.

So, why do it? Explore the alternative, which would be to tell the terrible truth with those four, tiny, very-tough-to-say words:

I made a mistake.

And add to that four even more useful words: *I learned from it.*

And four more: *It won't happen again.*

When you admit a mistake, declare you learned from the experience, and resolve that it won't happen again, you not only have put yourself on the momentary Pedestal of Truth, you have shown you possess two great lasting character traits: You tell the truth and you are a humility junkie.

Too many managers think humility has something to do with humiliation. In reality, it is a sign of courage. Only one person can create an environment of humiliation for you, and that's you. Lying and getting caught—that's humiliation.

Humility and honesty are the new courage. Pass it on.

Isolation in the workplace inhibits professional and business growth.

46 • Four more words for the road

Leaders, by their titles, diverse responsibilities and schedules, most times find themselves isolated from the people who create the situations that made and will make them successful.

Great managers don't accept that as a normal way of doing business. They work around the hierarchy by understanding that while they are knowledgeable, they are not all-knowing; that although they are creative when it comes to ferreting out meaningful information, they cannot always find, and do not always have, all the answers to every problem or opportunity.

Great managers know sometimes the answers come from places where they didn't expect to find them.

A certain Fortune 500 CEO figured out early in his executive career that his time spent with line employees and mid-level managers had become scarce. How could he make time from his busy schedule to mix and mingle with those who worked hard to make him successful?

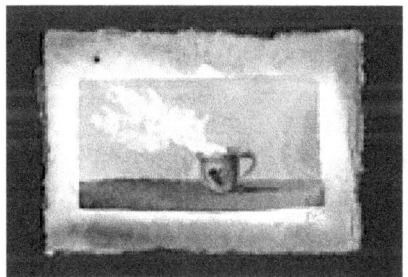

Sometimes the best ideas cost a pittance.

One day, a random thought took root. He usually ate lunch in the company cafeteria. So why couldn't he take advantage of the time and opportunity to learn more about his company?

Three or four times a month he would head to the cafeteria and board the elevator with employees heading the same direction. "Who is going to eat in the cafeteria?" he would ask.

Hands would go up.

Four words: *"I'll buy you lunch."*

Those lunches were nice breaks for the employees—lunch with the CEO usually is—but were better breaks for the CEO and the company he headed. After asking about each employee's responsibilities and hobbies and other chit-chat, he would pose to them this question: "If you could wave a magic wand and make one change in your department that would enable you to do a better job and create an opportu-

Fish for fresh and innovative ideas wherever you can find them.

nity—either in improving customer service, driving revenues, or saving on expenses—what would that change be?"

Besides giving employees opportunities to provide input on company procedures and protocol, thus building company loyalty and employee morale, the information he took from the lunch meetings was invaluable. The employee messages inevitably found their way into the corporation's boardroom, and emerged as new policies that strengthened the company.

Sometimes the best ideas sneak up on you from unexpected places.

Showing you have a heart is more positive than working hard to prove you don't have one

47 • When to lie

Here's a new experience you should try: Don't tell a single lie for an entire day. Tell yourself you want to be better than you are. Prostrate yourself to, well, *yourself.* Then, get the new you back to work and enjoy a lie-free day.

There's one area you can correct immediately: Don't lie to yourself. It's easy to lie to yourself, you know. People do it all the time.

The grocery store checker thought the snow peas were green beans. "What are these?" she asked. I told her I didn't know and she punched them in as green beans and I saved a bunch of money. I would have told her, but I didn't because the store didn't properly train her and she was just stupid.

You've probably done something similar at work—told a lie that was snow-white in color. You had a report due, but it fell into the Crack of Too Many Projects. You actually finished it, but were dis-

Lying and trying to cover it up is like being shot out of a cannon ... and then realizing you forgot to put up the safety net.

tracted by One Chore Too Many and didn't remember to send it via e-mail by the deadline. Then the boss reminded you and you lied that you sent it, when you didn't, and then had to try to figure out quickly how to make it look like you did.

"I know I sent it, because I found it in my outbox. The server must have slammed it. I just sent it to you again."

If you are going to lie, if you feel you have to lie, then lie to yourself and leave others out of it.

Humility and honesty are still the new courage. Pass it on. Again.

A human characteristic: Having dreams and aspirations.

48 • The dream's the thing

You are human. You have dreams about what you want to do, where you want to go, and how you want to manage your life, your relationships and your career.

Dreams are psychic carrots for your life. Keep them on the stick, out in front of you, always in your mind. Stay focused on their potential. Be proud of the images they project. Take them seriously, and nurture them.

Moving dreams from the surreal to reality is in no way self-induced illusion. In fact, it's an essential form of reality. Dreams are necessary to expand the reality of your self-imposed boundaries.

Dreams are not what you are, but what you could be—if you recognize the dreams for what they are: images that can be applied to your personal and professional lives.

Dream dreams others do not dare to dream. Refuse to let dreams die. To a breathing, thinking, caring person, dreams represent the best of what we have to give.

When a dream dies, so does a part of the dreamer.

You don't have to blindly follow the carrots offered by others. Provide your own.

49 • Be clear—very, very clear

Good managers tend to be clear in many ways. They are clear-headed and clear when they give advice and instructions. They are clear on what goals should be set and what paths should be followed, and very clear in their abilities to encourage total commitment from themselves and team members.

Great managers are just as clear in every respect. But they add an ingredient: They are also bold.

Having a bold plan of action and shouting it out, taking pathways others studiously avoid and looking for opportunities in places others have overlooked or ignored create the personality of a great manager.

Great managers don't start conversations with "I think," or "I know." They start with "I believe . . ."

To be clear, your view—and your views—must be uncluttered.

"I think" lacks commitment. "I know" leaves no room for doubt or consensual buy-in by team members. "I believe" is a strong statement of commitment, drawing in fellow believers, encouraging them. "I believe" can sway those who simply don't have an opinion.

When you state your beliefs emphatically, with reasonable arguments about why they are valid, you invite others to participate in the journey.

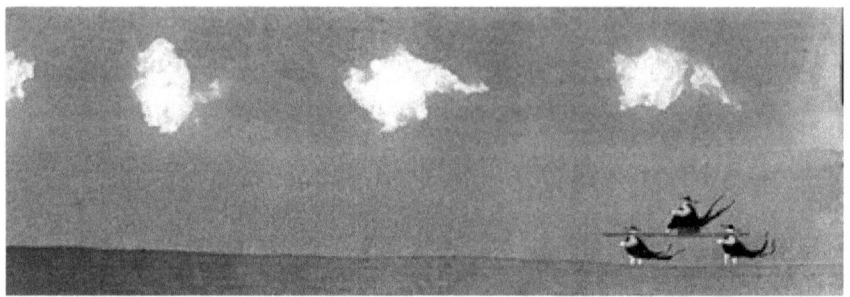

Working together, as a team, signifies strength.

50 • Strength in all things

To be strong is to be prepared. To be strong is to be steadfast. To be strong is never to give up. To be strong is to stand up for your beliefs, and stand shoulder-to-shoulder with those whose beliefs you embrace.

Be strong. Be a shoulder.

You are going to succeed on your merits, assuredly. But stop and pay homage to mentors, managers and leaders whose shoulders carried the load before you came along. Remember the shoulders you leaned on in your life, and pledge to be a strong shoulder for those who follow.

Be a shoulder and you will be an army of one.

Change often brings out the creativity in people.

51 • Cut your losses

L et's assume for a moment you are the Slurpee Manager at the corner convenience store. You are good at your job.

But at some point in your professional career, you determine you are too big for your job, and accept it as a psychological fact that your soul, ambitions, and drive to succeed are being crushed. The natural feeling at first, and a logical human assumption, is to look at yourself as a failure.

There comes a time in every person's career when he or she must admit, "This job is just not right for me!" It's not that you failed. It's that you finally took the time to look at your present situation dispassionately, and made a decision to change. That's an example of personal courage, an important step in the recognizing the *Circumference of Me*.

When faced with such a situation, you have three choices:

1) Don't do a thing and hope that some miracle appears and smites you, creating a rainbow of possibilities;

2) Don't do anything and know that someday soon you will be a hollow shell with a soul the size of a lentil; or

3) Start looking for the right business ladder to climb.

Suggestion: Go with No. 3. You and the company will benefit from the decision. It takes a lot of courage to face reality, to set new goals and make discernible changes in your life.

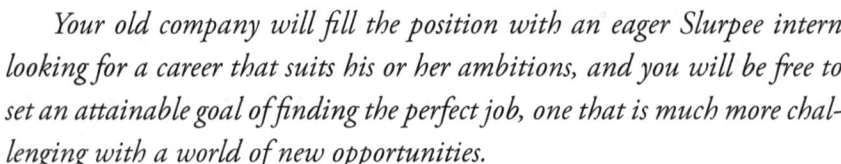

Your old company will fill the position with an eager Slurpee intern looking for a career that suits his or her ambitions, and you will be free to set an attainable goal of finding the perfect job, one that is much more challenging with a world of new opportunities.

52 • Bowling for kittens

It's inevitable that every once in a while, your mind will slip a gear and career downhill at a terrible pace. Keep such gear-slipping thoughts to a minimum, and remember: At those times, you have a choice: Suppress the thought, or go with the flow and see where you end up.

Creative juices flow differently in different people. For some, they spring forth like busted water lines. For others, they drip for a while before bursting into torrents. And for still others, they are like oscillating sprinklers—on, off, on, off.

Knowing how your creative juices flow and understanding how to turn them on and off at will is a gift that can be opened to its full potential over time.

What's the dumbest work-related idea you can think of? (Hey, we're not talking about going postal and ending the existence on this Earth of the office posterior slurper. Or going to the CEO and complaining about your supervisor, who just happens to be his brother-in-law. Those are not dumb thoughts. Those are stupid thoughts. Dumb can be corrected. Stupid is forever. Even two dumbs do not a stupid make.)

For example: You don't really want to implement an idea for something as stupid as "bowling for kittens." But if you follow that thought and turn it over in your mind, it might lead you to "bowling for cats," then to "bowling for cactus," then to "cactus bowls" and, finally, after four or more other thought mutations, to "selling miniature cactus to city dwellers." After you make your first million pushing off prickly pear cacti onto people living in small spaces, the idea won't seem so dumb, after all.

And you thought "bowling for kittens" was stupid.

"There's no such thing as an ugly baby or a dumb idea" would be considered a truism if there weren't some really ugly-ass babies out there. Work to keep the ideas others may think of as "dumb" to yourself until they ripen into something quite extraordinary. Don't throw the dumb ideas away; figure out how to make them work for you.

53 • Picking the right path

If you were an artist, would you be a Jackson Pollock or a Grandma Moses?

If you were a professional basketball player, would you rather be Michael Jordan or Robert Parrish?

If you were an auto racer, would you be Helio Castroneves or Tony Stewart?

If you are a manager, are you a micro, a macro, or a "Hands-off Ronald"?

People tend to gravitate to whatever is comfortable, whether in their present situations, their expectations of themselves, or others' expectations. One's personal comfort zone—in business and in life—depends on innumerable factors: genetics, upbringing, personal observations, education, and the general experiences one normally has in life.

Companies have levels of expectation, too, which fit their organizational models—all of which on some level, in some sense, are like wolf packs.

You couldn't expect a child reared in the wild by wolves to understand the intricacies of managing a complex corporate project. But you could expect the same child to understand the hierarchies of most companies and organizations. Such a child would know about alpha males and females, the roles of lesser players, and how one rises from a submissive role to one of dominance.

Some companies or associations don't want to seem at all like wolf packs. They openly disdain titles that put some employees on higher planes than others. These companies use ambiguous titles like "leader" instead of "director," "president," or "CEO." These same companies also eliminate the trappings of power—corner offices with majestic views, exotic coffee machines, executive washrooms—so their "leaders"

Having power is more than wishing for it, or thinking it will materialize on command.

can look like members of the pack.

The only ones they are fooling are themselves.

In every organization, every department, everyone knows who the alphas are. The absence of normally accepted titles of authority makes not one whit of difference in the normal corporate Order of Power. Who is in charge is evident; the alpha's status is known and acknowledged. It's part of the corporate culture, regardless of any claims otherwise.

Only you can decide what kind of manager you want to be, and where you will fit in the pack., and you may think you will know whether you have chosen the right path. But the true judges of what kind of manager you really are will be the people who work with you on three levels: those to whom you report, those with whom you work, and those who report to you.

You can try to be the next Jackson Pollock or try to emulate the style of Grandma Moses. You will fail. Seek your own comfort level in your organization and work hard to continually enhance your skills in order to expand your growth potential.

54 • Set the radar scan lower

We've discussed why some of the best ideas in businesses never get out of the mental closet. It's worth a closer look.

The best ideas floating around in the brain pans of a corporation's employees are never realized because either 1) employees don't have enough confidence to present their ideas for fear of ridicule, or 2) management doesn't encourage ideas from members of the workforce.

Too many managers don't believe they need input from others because they are cocksure they already know what works, what doesn't, what will happen, and what they will do when it does. These are the same managers who don't fish or hunt because they can't control their surroundings.

But what if an idea doesn't lay fallow?

A Fortune 500 company announced a contest to encourage employees to come up with ideas to generate revenue or cut expenses. One employee came up with an idea he said would save twelve dollars a day by creating a shortcut for customer service processes.

His supervisor pooh-poohed his suggestion at a managers' meeting to go over the entries, exclaiming: "Twelve dollars a day! This employee wants to save twelve dollars a day!"

A young manager on the selection team, just promoted from the rank and file, asked, "Don't we have more than 1,000 employees doing that same function?"

Bottom line: The company adopted the idea and within 60 days, savings of more than $12,000 a day were being realized. The company saved more than $500,000 the first year.

Sometimes the smallest ideas result in the biggest payoffs.

55 • Add a shark to the tank

As noted, your company, any company, has to change, evolve, go through a cultural metamorphosis in order to continue to grow and be viable in the marketplace.

Many companies disdain "change for change's sake," but constant, controlled change—which is decidedly different from corporate turmoil—can be helpful. It can keep a company fresh. In that case, change is not recognized as "change," but as an important foundation of the corporate culture.

But how much change is good change?

In the mid-1970s, venerated television newsman Walter Cronkite told the nation about an interesting group of Mexican fishermen working in the Gulf of Mexico.

In his patented been-there-done-that, competent manner, Cronkite reported that the live-catch fishermen would go out for three days. Then they had to head back to port, even if their live wells were not full.

Why? Three days was how long the fish could survive in the boat's "aquarium."

On top of that, despite all the precautions the fishermen took, their catches suffered an average attrition rate of twenty percent. Fiddling with temperature, water quality, oxygen and numbers made no difference. Even with everything just right, one-fifth of each boatload of fish died and became unfit to sell before they could make it home.

Twenty percent is pretty much the high end of the profit ratio for even the most price-aggressive companies.

As it happens with many great ideas and inventions, an accident solved the problem.

One day a fisherman inadvertently dropped a small shark into the tank along with the catch. When they got back to shore, the crew found no dead fish. It seems having a predator in the tank kept the fish swimming.

The threat of being eaten kept them alive.

Cronkite's report could just as easily have been about business. In your job, in your business, what might happen if you tossed a "shark" into the tank? What would happen if you took a creative spirit from, say, marketing or the graphic design area, to drop in among engineering, or cycled a marketer through the information technology group?

Disruptive measures, even ones usually thought of as counterproductive, might just keep the company moving, and alive.

You know the chapter above is not an advertisement for "Shark Week," right?

Good ideas don't necessarily have to be controlled. Some need to fly free.

56 • Birds of paradise in the business world

Ideas, like birds, come in all shapes, sizes, colors, and degrees of usefulness. Some fly on their own. Others need coaxing or pushing to realize their potential. Some are beautiful, but hard to catch and hold on to. Some are ugly at first sight but, with nurturing, will add immensely to the bottom line, or even the corporate culture.

Many managers believe they must control ideas so they can put their personal stamps on the outcomes, especially if they work. But what will happen when ideas are no longer caged in the owner's mind or abandoned to languish in a dreaded Corporate File? What happens when ideas are allowed to develop on their own, to seek their own way?

The sources of good ideas are as varied as the species of birds.

Good ideas can come from anywhere, from anyone.

The recent crisis in the American automotive industry was the

Good ideas, like caged birds, have a need to be free in order to sing.

topic at a sit-around of executives from a company with only periph-eral contact with auto manufacturing. Out of that discussion came this observation:

"Those yahoos in Detroit must be asleep at the mental wheel. The economic situation is pushing people toward electric and hybrid cars, and the car dealers are discouraging that segment of the market by mak-ing hybrid vehicles that are ass-ugly.

"Wonder if the boys at Ford have ever thought of making a fuel-efficient or electric vehicle that was an exact replica of the 1964 Mustang? Now, that baby would sell, for sure."

Good ideas can from anyone, anywhere. Look, listen, learn, surmise, and act when it's time for an idea to be set free.

57 • The 'music' of business

Christopher Walken's famous "Cowbell!" sketch on *Saturday Night Live* was about the music business. It could have been about any business.

Of course, you want your corporate orchestra members in tune. You want the saxophones to sound like saxophones, the flutes to make pleasant flute sounds, drums to sound drummy—you get the picture.

But when things seem to be in perfect pitch and rhythm, that's when you need a corporate Spike Jones to step in and beat a discordant rhythm on a cowbell or six.

If a business seems too perfect to be true, then it's either not perfect or not true. Businesses and departments are not machines, even if some executives and managers tend to want to run them like they are. A business, a department, has to be a living, breathing, dynamic, changing organism.

It would be nice if we could take a chore, project, department, and/

The winds of compromise and change make wonderful music.

or company and turn on the parts that make it work, then just watch it purr. However, that's simply not how business works.

A business has to be ever-changing because the market is constantly in flux. It has to be "alive" in order to change and grow. It has to be dynamic because the marketplace is dynamic.

Think of a business as a human body. It has to have parts that think, that work to control operations, that perform tasks, and that can contemplate changes in a calculated manner or move in a hurry to take advantage of opportunities.

The *body of business* is only as good as the sum of its parts. And it can only get better if someone, somewhere in the organization has the nerve to shout out: "Cowbell! I want more cowbell!" And someone else has the nerve to say: "Cowbell! Get him more cowbell!"

There's more to music than perfectly tuned instruments. It's the same with business. There are times when disharmony has a progressive rhythm.

Any business must be ready for change-winds that are constantly gusting.

Lastword

ook at the shape of your life, your career. Have you ever stopped to consider that what you see could be compared to a city skyline?

The makeup of a city has a stunning complexity that overwhelms the senses. The intricacies of the history of a city—how it began and where it ended up—paint in its skyline a portrait of dense, vibrant beauty, and constant change. You see your favorite city as a familiar pattern or patchwork of patterns, intricately woven by diverse people and the fads and trends thrust upon its inhabitants over time.

Every city, just like every person, is different, yet both are constructed from the same basic shapes.

Look at the skylines of New York, San Francisco, Dallas, Chicago or Des Moines. Look at them from above, via an Internet satellite image. You see different sizes of the same shapes—squares, circles, rectangles, and triangles. Give any dreamer, schemer, lord or lout these shapes, and in time a city will rise. The products will be direct results of their imaginations. That is quite simply how it works. Complexity rises out of some very simple pieces combined into shapes familiar.

So it is with your life. Its pieces are constructed of myriad images forged by genetics, traditions, education, experiences, imagination and dreams, plus scattered and concentrated creative thought. Together they make the *Circumference of Me.*

It takes a lifetime to grow a life. It can take a single bad economic moment or a horrific business decision to break it apart.

The pieces may lie at your feet, disconnected to present realities, jumbled into unrecognizable shapes with no matches, no fits. Concept to chaos—sometimes in an instant.

When that happens, you have two choices: despair or build. You get to choose, and no one can choose for you. But know this for certain: At this moment, it may be one of the few things in life you can control.

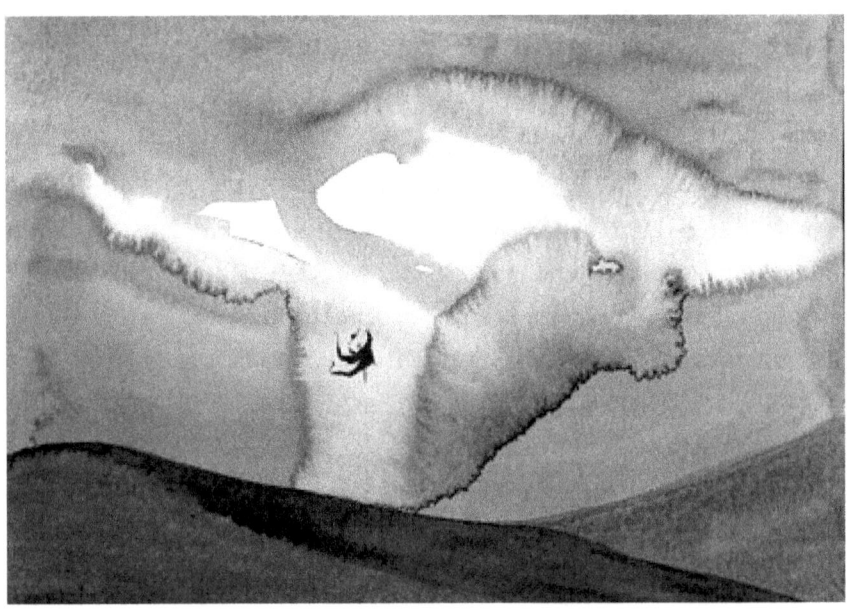

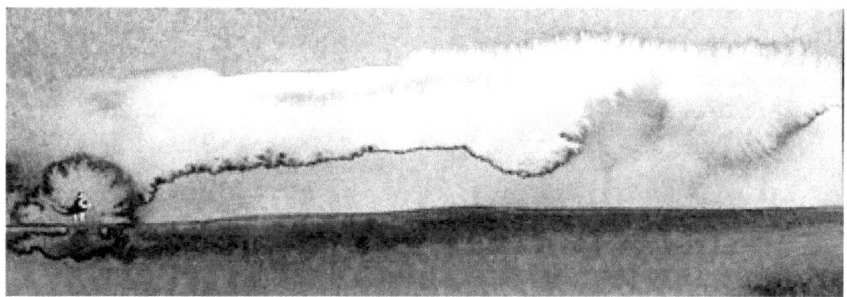

Despair or build?

The first option is easy. All you have to do is sit down and cry out your fears and excuses for all to hear. It takes a little energy, and an emotional toll but, really, not all that much of either. As a profession-building exercise, whining is a low-maintenance activity with few rewards. You just tell the little Optimist Man in your head to take a hike.

To build a city, or to construct or reconfigure a life, however, is a difficult undertaking. You not only have to lay aside your comfortable Robe of Poor Me, you have to think and plan and strategize, and set goals and a program of work, and get busy.

The main question is quite simple: How did you get where you are now, and where do you want to be in the future?

It takes designing, manufacturing, and managing individual pieces and parts to build a city, just as it does to build a life.

You can't build a city, or a life, in a day. You start by selecting a proper site and building a strong foundation, which should be anchored in the discovery and constant expansion of the Circumference of Me.

About the authors

Steve Burnett, president of the Burnett Group—a management, brand, and communications consulting company in New York City— is a professor of communications design at the Pratt Institute. His company's clients are Who's Who of global brand names. He's also an accomplished artist, and is creator of the "whimsy" style of art.

George S. Smith, director of communications services for Topcon Positioning Systems, is a writer, columnist, former newspaper editor and publisher, community development consultant, and national motivational speaker. He has taught management courses at the college level and has been a certified online instructor in strategic management and critical thinking.

Burnett and Smith are co-founders of Whimsy Creations LLC, a firm that develops unique fund-raising products combining "whimsy" drawings and poetry for small, non-profit organizations.

Circumference of Me